ELIJAH

A Man of Heroism and Humility

From the Bible-Teaching Ministry of
CHARLES R. SWINDOLL

INSIGHT FOR LIVING

Charles R. Swindoll graduated in 1963 from Dallas Theological Seminary, where he now serves as the school's fourth president, helping to prepare a new generation of men and women for the ministry. Chuck has served in pastorates in three states: Massachusetts, Texas, and California, including almost twenty-three years at the First Evangelical Free Church in Fullerton, California. He is currently senior pastor of Stonebriar Community Church in Frisco, Texas, north of Dallas. His sermon messages have been aired over radio since 1979 as the *Insight for Living* broadcast. A best-selling author, he has written numerous books and booklets on many subjects.

Based on the outlines, charts, and transcripts of Charles R. Swindoll's sermons, in 1992 the Bible study guide was coauthored by David Lien, a graduate of Dallas Theological Seminary. In 2001 this guide was revised and expanded by the Pastoral Ministries Department of Insight for Living.

Editor in Chief:
Cynthia Swindoll

Study Guide Writer:
David Lien

Senior Editor and Assistant Writer:
Wendy Peterson

Editors:
Connie Laser
Glenda Schlahta
Christianne Varvel

Rights and Permissions:
The Meredith Agency

Text Designer:
Gary Lett

Graphic System Administrator:
Bob Haskins

Director, Communications Division:
John Norton

Print Production Manager:
Don Bernstein

Print Buyer:
Becki Sue Gómez

Unless otherwise identified, all Scripture references are from the New American Standard Bible, updated edition, copyright © The Lockman Foundation 1960, 1962, 1963, 1968, 1971, 1972, 1973, 1975, 1977, 1995. Used by permission. Scripture taken from the Holy Bible, New International Version, Copyright © 1973, 1978, 1984 International Bible Society, used by permission of Zondervan Bible Publishers [NIV].

An effort has been made to locate sources and obtain permission where necessary for the quotations used in this book. In the event of any unintentional omission, a modification will gladly be incorporated in future printings.

ISBN 1-57972-352-7

Cover Design: Alex Pasieka. Adapted from the hardback cover design by D2 Design Works; hardback illustration by David Bowers.

Printed in the United States of America

CONTENTS

INTRODUCTION

Few people were more significant to or feared by the ancient Jews than those who stood before the people as God's prophets. When they spoke, the people listened. The prophets' words drilled their way into the heart, and though their message wasn't always appreciated, it could not be ignored.

No one would deny that Elijah was one of the greatest prophets. A man of both heroism and humility, he was God's lightning during the dark days under Ahab and Jezebel's rule. He appeared on the scene suddenly . . . and he disappeared with a flash of God's power into the sky. But in between his entrance and exit, Elijah etched an indelible mark upon his times.

In no way, however, should we think of him as superhuman. As James wrote in his letter, "Elijah was a man with a nature like ours" (5:17). His life was a window on God's power and heart—like ours should be. But he had his weaknesses too, just like us. Hopefully, as we identify with Elijah's humanity, we'll also grow to understand more about God's care for him . . . and His care for us.

So let's listen and learn. Elijah's life and times are as relevant to this generation as those whose names appear in today's newspaper. Perhaps more so!

Chuck Swindoll

Charles R. Swindoll

PUTTING TRUTH INTO ACTION

K nowledge apart from application falls short of God's desire for His children. He wants us to apply what we learn so that we will change and grow. This Bible study guide was prepared with these goals in mind. As you go through the following pages, we hope your desire to discover biblical truth will grow as your understanding of God's Word increases, and that you will be encouraged to apply what you've learned.

To assist you in your study, we've included a section called Living Insights at the end of each lesson. These exercises will challenge you to study further and to think of specific ways to put your discoveries into action.

In this edition, we've added Questions for Group Discussion, which are formulated to get your group talking about the key issues in each lesson.

On occasion a lesson is followed by a Digging Deeper section, which gives you additional information and resources to probe further into some issues raised in that lesson.

There are many ways to use this guide—in personal devotions, group studies, discussions with friends and family, and Sunday school classes. And, of course, it's an ideal study aid when you're listening to its corresponding *Insight for Living* radio series.

To benefit most from this Bible study guide, we would encourage you to consider it a spiritual journal. That's why we've included space in the **Living Insights** for recording your thoughts and discoveries. We hope you'll return to those sections often for review and encouragement as you continue to grow in your walk with Christ.

Insight for Living

ELIJAH

A Man of Heroism and Humility

Chapter 1

STANDING ALONE IN THE GAP
1 Kings 16:29–17:1

O f all the prophets who blazed across ancient Israel's history, none burned as radiantly as Elijah.

J. Oswald Sanders likened him to a meteor that "flashed across the inky blackness of Israel's spiritual night."[1] And Matthew Henry wrote that

> never was Israel so blessed with a good prophet as when it was so plagued with a bad king. Never was king so bold to sin as Ahab; never was prophet so bold to reprove and threaten as Elijah. . . . He only, of all the prophets, had the honor of Enoch, the first prophet, to be translated, that he should not see death, and the honor of Moses, the great prophet, to attend our Savior in his transfiguration. Other prophets prophesied and wrote, he prophesied and acted, but wrote nothing; but his actions cast more luster on his name than their writings did on theirs.[2]

Who was Elijah? And what set him apart? To gain an understanding of this fiery prophet, whose comet trail we'll be tracing through the next ten studies, we must first understand the times in which he lived.

The Times of Elijah

The steel of a person's character is forged on the anvil of one's times. And often, the darker the times are, the more brightly shines the soul that stands against them.

---

1. J. Oswald Sanders, *Robust in Faith* (Chicago, Ill.: Moody Press, 1965), p. 125.

2. Matthew Henry, *Commentary on the Whole Bible*, one-volume ed. (Grand Rapids, Mich.: Zondervan Publishing House, Regency Reference Library, 1961), p. 385.

We need only think of such people as Abraham Lincoln, steering our country through the darkness of the Civil War; Winston Churchill, rallying England—and the world—to never give in until the deep night of Nazism was broken through; and Martin Luther King Jr., showing generations how to overcome hate and injustice with dignity and resolve.

These were bright lights in decadent times, brilliant stars cast against a darkened sky. And few skies were darker in Israel's history than the one against which Elijah flung his faith.

Generally—the Kings of Israel

Saul, David, and Solomon, each in their turn, had ruled a unified Hebrew nation for more than one hundred years. But when Solomon's son Rehoboam ascended the throne, he foolishly oppressed the people with heavy taxes and conscription labor, which prompted a north-south division (1 Kings 12:1–24). The northern people were known as Israel, while the southerners were called Judah. This Israel-Judah distinction carries through Scripture until Israel (the north) is defeated by the Assyrians and Judah (the south) is sacked by Babylon. This period between the split and the Babylonian captivity is known as the time of the kings. Some of those kings were good; most were evil.

A brief survey of the northern kings leading up to Elijah's time will show us what this man of God was up against.

Jeroboam. While Rehoboam continued to rule Judah, Jeroboam became the first king of the new northern nation of Israel. An evil man, he led the people away from God and into idolatry:

> He made priests of the high places from among all the people; any who would, he ordained, to be priests of the high places. This event became sin to the house of Jeroboam, even to blot it out and destroy it from off the face of the earth. (13:33b–34)

Jeraboam's legacy of murder, deception, and religious perversion ran throughout the entire line of Israel's kings.

Nadab. This son of Jeroboam fanned the same idolatrous coals his father had lit.

> He did evil in the sight of the Lord, and walked in the way of his father and in his sin which he made Israel sin. (15:26)

Nadab's two-year reign ended with his murder (v. 27).

Baasha. After killing Nadab, Baasha wiped out anyone associated with Jeroboam's previous dynasty and established a twenty-four-year reign of evil (vv. 28–29, 33):

> He did evil in the sight of the Lord, and walked in
> the way of Jeroboam and in his sin which he made
> Israel sin. (v. 34)

Elah. While in a drunken stupor, this son of Baasha was assassinated by his servant Zimri after only two short years of rule:

> Zimri destroyed all the household of Baasha . . .
> for all the sins of Baasha and the sins of Elah his
> son, which they sinned and which they made Israel
> sin, provoking the Lord God of Israel to anger with
> their idols. (16:12–13)

Zimri. Having murdered the king and all his house and Baasha's house, Zimri was next to sit on Israel's throne. What followed is incredible. Zimri ruled for only one week before the people begged Omri, the commander of the army, to be their king (vv. 15–16). He complied and laid siege to Zimri's city; and Zimri, in desperation, committed suicide (vv. 17–18). Scripture's same mournful refrain sums up Zimri's life like the rest:

> He sinned, doing evil in the sight of the Lord, walk-
> ing in the way of Jeroboam, and in his sin which he
> did, making Israel sin. (v. 19)

Tibni. The path to Israel's throne was not smooth for Omri. Though half the nation clamored for him to be king, the other half wanted Tibni. The two men co-reigned until

> the people who followed Omri prevailed over the
> people who followed Tibni the son of Ginath. And
> Tibni died and Omri became king. (v. 22)

Omri. Finally, after besieging one king and overpowering another, Omri got his chance to step up to the throne. Though he brought some semblance of stability to Israel, he never sought the Lord. In fact, he exceeded all his predecessors in evil acts:

> Omri did evil in the sight of the Lord, and acted
> more wickedly than all who were before him. For
> he walked in all the way of Jeroboam the son of

Nebat and in his sins which he made Israel sin, provoking the Lord God of Israel with their idols. (vv. 25–26)

For more than half a century, intrigue, bloodshed, conspiracy, and immorality permeated Israel's social infrastructure. And for all of those years, the insidious tendrils of idolatry slowly spread over the nation and sunk their roots down deep.

The darkness was terrible, but it was about to get worse as Omri's son Ahab ascended the throne.

Specifically—Ahab and Jezebel . . . and Baal

Ahab has a unique distinction in the annals of the kings.

Ahab the son of Omri did evil in the sight of the Lord more than all who were before him.

It came about, as though it had been a trivial thing for him to walk in the sins of Jeroboam the son of Nebat, that he married Jezebel the daughter of Ethbaal king of the Sidonians, and went to serve Baal and worshiped him. So he erected an altar for Baal in the house of Baal which he built in Samaria. Ahab also made the Asherah. Thus Ahab did more to provoke the Lord God of Israel than all the kings of Israel who were before him. (vv. 30–33)

The account of Ahab's reign is also the first among the kings to elaborate on a marriage (v. 31). And for good reason.

By himself Ahab would have been a menace. . . . Plainly an opportunist, he seems to have had few convictions or scruples. But he was not by himself. Jezebel was by his side, using her prestige and influence as insidiously and maliciously as possible. Like Solomon's foreign wives, she continued her pagan worship, maintaining it on a lavish scale. When the prophets of Yahweh opposed her heathen ways, she set out viciously to destroy them, ruthlessly and thoroughly. . . .

Having bent every effort to suppress true prophetic activity, Jezebel imported to her court hundreds of false prophets dedicated to Baal. . . . Such zeal in so strategic a position posed an incalculable

4

threat to Israel's historic faith. The corruption of Canaanite religion had long been seeping in from the Israelites' Canaanite neighbors, but under Jezebel it was pumped from the palace with extraordinary pressure.[3]

Jezebel, her name long synonymous with wickedness, would be Elijah's chief human foe—for it was she who ruled her husband and, therefore, the nation. Her god Baal, however, represented the spiritual enemy who threatened to steal the souls of the people from their one true God, Yahweh.

In order to show beyond any doubt who the true God is, the Lord would perform specific miracles through Elijah's ministry geared to undermine every one of Baal's so-called powers. Just what sort of a god was Baal? He was the Canaanites' chief fertility god as well as the storm god in charge of rain, wind, and clouds—which would definitely impact the fertility of crops. His followers gave him many titles: Rider of the Clouds; Prince, Lord of the Earth; Lord of Rain and Dew; Lord of the Heavens; Master; Lord; Husband.[4] Ancient statues show him gripping a lightning bolt in his left hand, ready to hurl it as a spear toward earth, and thunder was his voice.[5] He was also symbolized as a bull, which represented his virile fertility. Degrading sexual acts were one way his followers worshiped him. Old Testament scholar Gene Rice explains:

> Baal was thought to be indispensable to vitality in nature. When the earth languished for want of rain

3. William Sanford LaSor, David Allan Hubbard, and Frederic William Bush, *Old Testament Survey* (Grand Rapids, Mich.: William B. Eerdmans Publishing Co., 1982), p. 266.

4. See Kurt Gerhard Jung, "Baal," in *The International Standard Bible Encyclopedia*, rev. ed. (1979; reprint, Grand Rapids, Mich.: William B. Eerdmans Publishing Co., 1988), vol. 1, pp. 377–78; A. E. Cundall, "Baal," in *The Zondervan Pictorial Encyclopedia of the Bible*, gen. ed. Merrill C. Tenney (Grand Rapids, Mich.: Zondervan Publishing House, Regency Reference Library, 1976), vol. 1, pp. 431–33; "Baal," in www.britannica.com, the online version of the *Encyclopædia Britannica*; J. Robinson, *The First Book of Kings*, The Cambridge Bible Commentary Series (London, England: Cambridge University Press, 1972), pp. 195–96; Thomas L. Constable, "1 Kings," in *The Bible Knowledge Commentary*, Old Testament edition, ed. John F. Walvoord and Roy B. Zuck (Colorado Springs, Colo.: Chariot Victor Publishing, 1985), p. 522; and Paul R. House, *1, 2 Kings*, The New American Commentary Series (Nashville, Tenn.: Broadman and Holman Publishers, 1995), vol. 8, pp. 210–11.

5. Raymond B. Dillard, *Faith in the Face of Apostasy: The Gospel according to Elijah and Elisha*, The Gospel according to the Old Testament Series (Phillipsburg, N.J.: Presbyterian and Reformed Publishing, 1999), pp. 5–6.

it was because Baal was slain by Mot, the god of sterility and death. When life was restored to nature it was because Baal was rescued and revived by his sister Anath, the goddess of love and war. Fertility was understood as a divine force released by sexual union between Baal and his consort, variously identified in the OT as Asherah . . . or Ashtoreth. . . . . The divine couple could be activated from the human realm by sexual relations with a cult prostitute.[6]

Delusion and degradation—Ahab and Jezebel's gifts to Israel. These are what God wanted to rescue His people from. And Elijah was His chosen representative in this showdown of the Gods.

The Person of Elijah

Into this dark scene stepped Elijah, who was not afraid to shine the light of God's word straight into Ahab's eyes:

Now Elijah the Tishbite, who was of the settlers of Gilead, said to Ahab, "As the Lord, the God of Israel lives, before whom I stand, surely there shall be neither dew nor rain these years, except by my word." (17:1)

"There is one God—Yahweh—and He is Israel's true God," Elijah asserted to the Baal-serving king. With these first words out of his mouth, Elijah had thrown down the gauntlet before Ahab. Who was this person who challenged Israel's royal couple? Just a man—not a superman—but a man who loved God more than his own life.

His Name

Elijah's name encapsulates his life's focus, authority, and message. Meaning "my God is Yahweh," his name

states succinctly the theme of his ministry. In an age characterized by easy tolerance and open assimilation to Canaanite religion, Elijah asserts his personal de-

---

6. Gene Rice, *Nations under God: A Commentary on the Book of 1 Kings*, International Theological Commentary Series (Grand Rapids, Mich.: William B. Eerdmans Publishing Co., 1990), p. 132.

termination ("My God" is emphatic) to keep the First Commandment. It is to bring the northern kingdom to a like determination that his ministry is directed.[7]

His Land

Elijah was a "Tishbite, who was of the settlers of Gilead" (v. 1). Though no one knows for sure anymore where Tishbe was located, we do have information about Gilead. This area east of the Jordan River is known for its ruggedness—rocky mountains, thickly wooded hills, and flatter regions replete with olive trees and vineyards define this region. It is a solitary place; many people, such as Jacob and David, sought refuge there. Gilead's ruggedness is reflected in Elijah's leathery character—tough, unpolished, humble. And yet Elijah was a man of compelling tenderness, which we shall see as his life unfolds in the studies to come.

His Style

Elijah's speech to Ahab in verse 1b reveals his style:

> "As the Lord, the God of Israel lives, before whom I stand, surely there shall be neither dew nor rain these years, except by my word."

Authoritative and to the point, Elijah's words show him to be a man zealous for and dedicated to God.[8] The Lord was more real to him than all the opposition of his day. He stood in the gap on behalf of God and His people (compare Ezek. 22:30) and made the clear voice of the Lord heard.

So few of us stand as Elijah did. We have learned, consciously or unconsciously, the way of the chameleon—we blend ourselves into the scenery of our times. Often our tolerance and long-suffering border on compromise, making us ineffective as Christ's lights in a dark world. But we needn't stay in that obscurity. We can learn, like Elijah, to flash "across the inky blackness" of our times and light up the sky with God's message of righteousness and love.

7. Rice, *Nations under God*, p. 141.

8. "Before whom I *stand*," *amad* in Hebrew, is "an expression of dedication, allegiance, and servitude" to Yahweh. R. Laird Harris, Gleason L. Archer Jr., and Bruce K. Waltke, eds., *Theological Wordbook of the Old Testament* (Chicago, Ill.: Moody Press, 1980), vol. 2, p. 674.

Lessons from Elijah

Elijah's life is rich with lessons for us; in fact, from this introduction alone, we can glean at least three.

God looks for special people at difficult times. God found Elijah, not among the royal family nor among anyone near Ahab or Jezebel, but in the rugged, remote terrain of Gilead. Position, power, connections, the "alphabet soup of academic degrees"[9]—none of these are God's criteria for choosing a servant. Rather, He looks for individuals who are ready instruments—those who stand out brightly against the backdrop of corrupt times (see 2 Chron. 16:9; Phil. 2:15).

God's methods are often surprising. One person, not an army, was sufficient to confront the entire Israelite government. God could have orchestrated another inside assassination, but that would not have revealed His heart for His people. Instead, He chose Elijah. Elijah, all alone, was the best strategy to use against the wicked king and his wife because of his uncompromising loyalty to God. Have you ever thought that perhaps you are God's chosen method in His unconventional warfare?

God wants us to stand before Him, first and foremost. Because Elijah was ever conscious of God's presence, he was able to face Ahab without fear. We, too, can face our Ahabs without fear, if we will irradiate our souls with an Elijah-like perspective of our Lord.

As we trace the star streaks of Elijah's life in the days ahead, let the Creator of light, the Light of the World, burn brightly in your heart so that you illumine your dark and stumbling world, as Elijah did his.

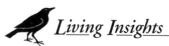 *Living Insights*

Our minds think funny things in the dark, don't they? Remember when you were a child and you had to take the trash out at night—when it was pitch black? You stepped out of the house's warm light and ventured into territory that, just hours earlier, was daylight-safe. But that same area was completely transformed by the dark into a world of monsters lurking behind corners, trees, and bushes.

---

9. Dillard, *Faith in the Face of Apostasy,* p. 16.

As Christians, we sometimes feel this way when we leave our softly-lit sanctuaries and venture out into the world. The terrors of *that* night, however, are quite real.

What are some areas of darkness in your society that frighten you?

_____ _____

_____ _____

_____ _____

Does your mind do funny things in the midst of this darkness? Sometimes we are paralyzed by fear or, worse, hardened by hopeless indifference. What thoughts and feelings surface when you encounter the situations you listed?

_____

_____

_____

In Ahab and Jezebel's day, God found someone to stand in the gap in dark and fearful times: Elijah. How about in your day?

Our sanctuaries are safe places—and rightly so. But the whole of a Christian's life can't be lived in the sanctuary; it must also be lived in the world. Are you willing, as Elijah was, to stand in the gap and pierce the darkness with the light of God's message? In what spheres can you begin to do this?

_____

_____

_____

_____

As you explore this question, take along some encouragement from the apostle John: "You are from God, little children, and have overcome them; because greater is He who is in you than he who is in the world" (1 John 4:4).

And learn from Elijah what one willing life in God's hands can do. In fact, as you begin this study, set aside some time to get to know this prophet on your own. Read 1 Kings 17–19, 21; 2 Kings 1–2; Matthew 17:1–8; Luke 9:28–36; and James 5:17–18. Get acquainted with this meteoric man through whom God will speak to you in the days ahead!

 Questions for Group Discussion

1. Do you see any similarities between your times and the times in which Elijah lived? What problems and areas of darkness seem to transcend time and afflict all ages?

2. We may not worship Baal anymore, but we still have present-day idols. What are the names of the idols in your society?

3. Have you ever been tempted to serve one of these idols? Money, for example, or materialism, pleasure, power, beauty, or youth? What forces in society foster this idolatry?

4. How have you been able to stand against these pressures? What helps you resist the temptations the world lays before you and keep your eyes fixed on the one true God?

5. Why do you suppose God bothered to send a prophet to such an evil, unfaithful society? Why didn't He simply wipe them out with a fiery blast of judgment? What does God's *not* doing this tell you about His character?

6. Elijah did not come from a prestigious family. He was not super-educated. He didn't hail from an important city. God brought him from obscurity to center stage in the drama He was directing. He did the same, in fact, with His own Son, Jesus Christ. And He does the same with us too (see 1 Cor. 1:26–28). You may not be called to be another Elijah, but God still wants you to be His light in a dark world. How do you let the light of Christ shine in your life?

Chapter 2

BOOT CAMP AT CHERITH

1 Kings 17:1–7

B *oot camp.* The very words conjure up images of freshly stubbled heads, dog tags, fatigues—and fatigue. Here civilians are molded into soldiers through the rigors of push-ups, sit-ups, running, and marching double-time, courtesy of the drill sergeant. Control of one's life is left at the induction center, and raw recruits are shaped into military fitness at another's hands.

As tough as this training is, there really isn't any other way to achieve the desired—and necessary—results. You just don't learn how to survive on a battlefield by bubbling around in a Jacuzzi!

To a certain extent, what's true in military life is also true in spiritual life. Unless we go through times of training—"boot camp" lessons on how to live as God's people, not the world's—we won't be able to accomplish the Lord's objectives and withstand Satan's assaults against us.

Even a prophet as great as Elijah needed additional training, which he got from the Lord in the solitary ravine of Cherith. But his story begins with a declaration of drought, which was really a declaration of war—Yahweh's war on Baal. Let's join him at Ahab's palace in Samaria, then follow him into his hiding place by the brook Cherith.

The Declaration of Drought

In a sudden, bold confrontation, Elijah delivered the Lord's message to King Ahab, Israel's spiritual *mis*leader.

> Now Elijah the Tishbite, who was of the settlers of Gilead, said to Ahab, "As the Lord, the God of Israel lives, before whom I stand, surely there shall be neither dew nor rain these years, except by my word." (1 Kings 17:1)

Drought. Elijah's was a harsh prophecy, but what better way to show the falsity of Baal, the rain and fertility god, than by the true Lord taking away the rain? This strategy would

> attack Baalism at its theological center. Baal worshipers believed that their storm god made rain,

11

unless, of course, it was the dry season and he needed to be brought back from the dead. To refute this belief Elijah states that Yahweh is the one who determines when rain falls, that Yahweh lives at all times, and that Yahweh is not afraid to challenge Baal on what his worshipers consider his home ground.[1]

Elijah also prophesied that the dew that kept the plants alive in summer would also fail. For how long? "These years"—not a few weeks, not a few months, but *years*. Farms would fail, famine would strike the land, and people would suffer.

What leader wants his religion proven wrong or his reign threatened with economic ruin? Not Ahab! So the Lord warned Elijah to hide in a remote place where He would keep him safe.

The Provision of Cherith

> The word of the Lord came to him, saying, "Go away from here and turn eastward, and hide yourself by the brook Cherith,[2] which is east of the Jordan. It shall be that you will drink of the brook, and I have commanded the ravens to provide for you there." So he went and did according to the word of the Lord, for he went and lived by the brook Cherith, which is east of the Jordan. (1 Kings 17:2–5)

Even though it may have looked like he tucked tail and ran, Elijah trusted his Lord and obeyed without question.

---

1. Paul R. House, *1, 2 Kings*, The New American Commentary Series (Nashville, Tenn.: Broadman and Holman Publishers, 1995), vol. 8, p. 213. The Lord would also have been upholding the covenant He made with Moses and all Israel: If they obeyed Him, He promised to bless them with rain, bountiful crops, and prosperity; but if they forsook Him, He promised to "make the rain of your land powder and dust" (see Deut. 28:1, 11–12, 15, 23–24). See Raymond B. Dillard, *Faith in the Face of Apostasy: The Gospel according to Elijah and Elisha*, The Gospel according to the Old Testament Series (Phillipsburg, N.J.: Presbyterian and Reformed Publishing, 1999), p. 17.

2. No one really knows anymore where the brook Cherith is located. "It has been thought to be the Wadi el-Kelt a few miles north of Jericho. But the Wadi el-Kelt is on the western side of the Jordan. This both contradicts the narrative and defeats the purpose of the hideaway, which was to be outside the jurisdiction of Ahab and therefore beyond his grasp. Another suggestion is the Wadi Yabis on the east side of the Jordan." J. Robinson, *The First Book of Kings*, The Cambridge Bible Commentary Series (London, England: Cambridge University Press, 1972), p. 200.

Hidden by a Brook

God always has a method in His mystery, and He had at least three purposes for Elijah's campout at Cherith. The Lord's first reason was to protect Elijah. After Ahab conveyed Elijah's message to Jezebel, she initiated a bloodbath against Yahweh's prophets (1 Kings 18:4). And when Ahab couldn't find Elijah, he left "no nation or kingdom" unturned in his manhunt (v. 10). So God sent Elijah to a safe place, because, as Gene Rice notes, "this was not the time to risk arrest and execution; Elijah must be free to interpret the meaning of the drought and bring it to an end." [3]

Second, Elijah's withdrawal also conveyed God's displeasure with the idolatrous people. Rather than "shine His face on" them (see Num. 6:22–27; Ps. 31:16; 80), He hid His face from them (compare Deut. 31:16–18; Ps. 27:9; 104:27–30; Mic. 3:4). Raymond Dillard observes, "Now Israel would endure not simply a famine of food and water, but a famine of the word of God (Amos 8:11; Ps. 74:9)." [4]

And third, God sent Elijah to Cherith for an additional time of training. Here the prophet was alone with God in the Lord's "boot camp," building the muscles of his faith by learning to depend solely on God's provision and protection. Ronald S. Wallace explains that Elijah's time by the brook also included lessons in the harsh realities of leadership.

> He was now involved himself, like Moses and Samuel before him, in the leadership of God's people. He will therefore have to become used to loneliness and rejection. He will have to be prepared for the coming experience of facing the nation with the feeling and belief that no one else around him knows, or understands, or cares for what to him are matters of life or death. . . . Elijah was later given an Elisha to attend him, but his main work was always accomplished pioneering alone. Here at Cherith he is being

---

3. Gene Rice, *Nations under God: A Commentary on the Book of 1 Kings*, International Theological Commentary Series (Grand Rapids, Mich.: William B. Eerdmans Publishing Co., 1990), p. 142.

4. Dillard, *Faith in the Face of Apostasy*, p. 21; see also Richard D. Patterson and Hermann J. Austel, "1 and 2 Kings," in *The Expositor's Bible Commentary*, gen. ed. Frank E. Gaebelein (Grand Rapids, Mich.: Zondervan Publishing House, Regency Reference Library, 1988), vol. 4, p. 138.

trained in the apartness that is to be such a charac-
teristic of his future life.[5]

Fed by Ravens

Elijah also learned some lessons from the ravens God commanded to share their meals with him:

> The ravens brought him bread and meat in the
> morning and bread and meat in the evening, and
> he would drink from the brook. (1 Kings 17:6)

While the rest of Israel was hungry and thirsty, God made sure
Elijah had enough to eat and drink. Like Moses before him, who
ate manna in the desert and drank water from a rock, so now Elijah
would see—every day—God's provision and power over His creation. What a vivid picture for us today of the truth that *God will
provide!* He knows our needs and tenderly meets them, as Jesus
reminded us:

> "Consider the ravens, for they neither sow nor reap;
> they have no storeroom nor barn, and yet God feeds
> them; how much more valuable you are than the
> birds!" (Luke 12:24)

So Elijah camped out by Cherith, enjoying cool, clear water,
the ravens' catering,[6] and undisturbed communion with God. It
sounds idyllic, doesn't it? A bit lonely, yet very peaceful. But it
wasn't meant to last:

> It happened after a while that the brook dried up,
> because there was no rain in the land. (1 Kings 17:7)

5. Ronald S. Wallace, *Readings in 1 Kings* (Grand Rapids, Mich.: William B. Eerdmans
Publishing Co., 1995), pp. 110–11.

6. According to Mosaic Law, ravens were "unclean" birds (Lev. 11:13–19). They eat just
about anything, from berries, seeds, and acorns to rodents, birds' eggs, and carrion. What an
interesting diet Elijah must have had! But what crucial lessons God was teaching. The Lord's
rules were made for people; His people were not made for the rules (see Mark 2:23–28).
God will accomplish His purposes through whomever, or whatever, He chooses. And He loves
and cares for all of His creation, "unclean" or not (compare Job 38:41; Ps. 147:9)—Israelite
(or Christian) or not. This last lesson would have been especially important for Elijah to
learn, because when the brook at Cherith dried up, God provided a Gentile woman in Jezebel's
own Canaanite homeland to take care of him (1 Kings 17:9). God's kingdom is meant to
draw everyone in (compare Luke 4:25–27; 10:30–37; Acts 10:1–11:18; Gal. 3:28–29).

Elijah had prayed that it would not rain (James 5:17), he had prophesied that it would not rain, and now he, too, was feeling the effects of no rain. He could have been hardened by moral indignation at the people's idolatry, proudly pronouncing judgment and coldly condemning sinners. But that wouldn't have reflected God's heart. So Elijah had to learn to empathize with the people, and that came through feeling what they were feeling. As Ronald Wallace explains,

> A feature of all effective leadership in the Old Testament is always its sympathy with, and understanding of, those who were called to follow. . . . God made sure that, even in his apartness, Elijah the future leader was brought into the closest contact with the suffering and feelings of those he had been sent by God to serve and pray for, and whose existence had been so bitterly affected by the word he had spoken.[7]

As we'll see in the next chapter, Elijah's compassion will be deepened further when he stays with a widow and her son in Zarephath, but the melting of his heart began at Cherith.

Some Lessons from Cherith

Can you imagine how you would have felt in Elijah's shoes as he watched the brook gradually dry up? God had told him to go to Cherith, and he had swiftly obeyed the Lord. Was this part of God's plan? He knew it was, and that this was no oversight on God's part. But do we know that when God places us beside drying brooks? Far from forgetting us, God is actually keenly aware of and active in our development, and He uses times likes these to teach us eternal lessons. Let's consider six lessons we can glean from Cherith-type experiences.

First, *the God who gives water can choose to take it away.* This is God's sovereign right. We often feel, however, that once He gives water, He should never take it back. Once He gives a spouse, a child, a business, or a ministry, we want it to be ours to keep. And when He takes it, we think He's suddenly turned against us. But God's sovereignty doesn't rule out His care. The most tender human

---

7. Wallace, *Readings in 1 Kings*, p. 111.

love may fail, but God will not forget us—"Behold, I have inscribed you on the palms of My hands" (Isa. 49:14–16).

Second, *our dried-up brooks can be the direct result of our own prayers.* Day by day, Elijah watched a flowing brook slowly dwindle into damp earth. What he was really seeing, though, was prophecy realized and prayer answered. He had "prayed earnestly that it would not rain, and it did not rain on the earth for three years and six months" (James 5:17). Most likely, he wasn't surprised by what he saw. But how often we are! It helps to remember what we've prayed for, doesn't it? Christlikeness, maturity, patience, and humility usually come through a Cherith kind of experience, not a weekend at the spa.

Third, *we must be as willing to be hidden as to be out in front.* F. B. Meyer saw in Elijah's time at Cherith "the value of the hidden life. . . . Every saintly soul that would wield great power with people must win it in some hidden Cherith. We cannot give out unless we have previously taken in."[8] We don't like to be hidden, though, do we? We often interpret it as being set aside, useless. But there is value in that hidden time. Even though we aren't on "active duty," God is still actively shaping our characters and preparing us for the next step in His plan.

Fourth, *God's direction includes provision.* God told Elijah to go to the brook, and when he got there he found safety, quietness, cool water, and a menu planned by ravens. Not exactly the chefs we would have chosen, but who better to find and carry food unnoticed to a remote hiding place—and who wouldn't tell a soul? God's ways of providing often surprise us, but they are always the best ways.

Fifth, *we are to trust God one day at a time.* Did you notice that God never told Elijah the next step until he had taken the first? And even after he had taken that first step, God didn't direct him further until the effects of the drought had become visible in Cherith. All that time, the ravens brought him food every morning and evening; Elijah always had just what he needed. Remember what Jesus told us? "Do not worry about tomorrow; for tomorrow will care for itself" (Matt. 6:34). Our Father knows our needs, and He provides our bread—daily.

And finally, *a drying brook is often a sign of God's pleasure, not His disappointment.* Elijah had done nothing to bring about God's discipline. Cherith wasn't a punishment; it was a protection. But

---

8. F. B. Meyer, *Great Men of the Bible* (London, England: Marshall Pickering, 1990), p. 344.

he couldn't stay there forever; God had work for him to do. The drying brook was the Lord's way of saying it was time to move on, time to see what the Lord wanted to do next.

If you feel like you're sitting beside a drying brook, remember how tenderly God dealt with Elijah. And God hasn't changed, you know. He is "the same yesterday and today and forever" (Heb. 13:8), and His lovingkindness never fails (see Ps. 100:5).

Living Insights

Reflecting on Elijah's time at Cherith, A. W. Pink makes this application to our lives:

> Ah, my reader, the man whom the Lord uses has to be kept low. . . . How humbling! Alas, how little is man to be trusted: how little is he able to bear being put into the place of honor! How quickly self rises to the surface, and the instrument is ready to believe he is something more than an instrument. How sadly easy it is to make of the very service God entrusts us with a pedestal on which to display ourselves.[9]

A Cherith-type experience is hard for us, isn't it? One of the most difficult commands for us to hear and obey is the command to be alone . . . to stop our busyness . . . to get away from the spotlight. Yet this is an essential part of becoming a mature man or woman of God. The following diagram shows God's training method—and His goal. (Keep in mind that each line represents a barrier of resistance to God's instruction, and each space shows a stage of development God wants to take us through.)

9. Arthur W. Pink, *The Life of Elijah* (Swengel, Pa.: Bible Truth Depot, 1956), p. 41.

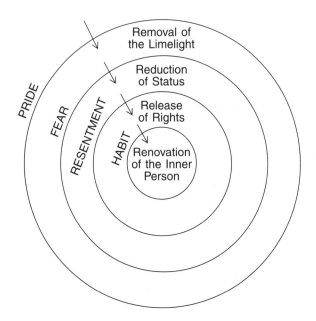

Before God can accustom us to His light, He must first remove the artificial limelight that pride shines in our eyes. Before God can bring us to nourishing pastures of humility, He must first take down the cardboard backdrop of status that our fears prop up. Before God can hand us the things He would give us freely, He must first pry our fingers loose from the rights our resentments hold fast. And before God can enlarge our hearts, He must first renew our inner person by breaking loose the habits that block the flow of life.

Where are you in God's training program? Is there a certain barrier you are struggling with? What has this been like for you? What has God taught you so far?

Though often challenging and sometimes painful, God's training method always has a purpose. It's to conform us to Christ's holy and loving image—and that's a goal that makes all our "boot camps" worthwhile.

 Questions for Group Discussion

1. Why was it so important for the Lord to "show up" Baal? What does it reveal about His care for His people? Does the drought seem to be the opposite of care? Why or why not?

2. God knew Elijah's life would be endangered by Ahab and Jezebel, so He told the prophet to hide. Has the Lord ever hidden you from harm? What was your experience? What did you learn about the Lord?

3. Ravens were "unclean" according to the Mosaic Law, and to some people, that may have meant they were not an acceptable means of provision. Can you think of scriptural examples of people who seemed "unacceptable," but whom God used to provide for His people? (If you need some help, look over a few of the names in Jesus' genealogy in Matthew 1.)

4. How open are you to God's sometimes unusual means of provision? Can you sense His care in a non-Christian's help? Or in the help of a person whose lifestyle is different from yours? Have you experienced this personally? If you're comfortable doing so, share what happened and what it was like.

5. Are you currently beside a "drying brook"? What is your brook? What do you think God is trying to teach you? How does Elijah's experience encourage you?

Chapter 3

ADVANCED TRAINING
AT ZAREPHATH

1 Kings 17:8–16

The brook Cherith, in its quiet loneliness, was both a refuge and a refinery for Elijah. Here he was hidden from Ahab and Jezebel, and here he was honed by isolation. Here his needs were met by God's provision, and here his brook dried up.

Was this the end of the road for Elijah? Would God leave His faithful servant beside a dry riverbed, letting his body and spirit become parched? No, not the God of answered prayers, fulfilled prophecy, and met needs. This was not the end of Elijah's road, but the beginning of another. For when that brook dried up,

> The word of the Lord came to him, saying, "Arise, go to Zarephath, which belongs to Sidon, and stay there; behold, I have commanded a widow there to provide for you." (1 Kings 17:8–9)

So to Zarephath Elijah went (v. 10a). And it is to Zarephath, where Elijah entered into more advanced training than at Cherith, that we will go to learn more about God's purposes and plans—for Elijah, for the widow, for Israel, and for us.

Experience at Zarephath

Why Zarephath? Before we delve any deeper into this episode of Elijah's life, let's explore the significance of his destination. Commentator Paul R. House explains that

> Zarephath is located in Phoenicia, the very heart of Baalism. Here Yahweh will defeat Baal in his own territory. Here God's people will fare better than Baal's. F. C. Fensham asserts that in fact the main purpose of this narrative is "to demonstrate on Phoenician soil, where Baal is worshiped, that Yahweh has power over things in which Baal has failed." Since Baal worshipers explained the drought as a sign that Baal was dead, he could not help the widow

20

and her son. "In the absence of Baal who lies impo-
tent in the Netherworld, Yahweh steps in to assist
the widow and the orphan. . . ." It is also done in
Jezebel's native land. Because Yahweh exists and
Baal does not, Elijah possesses power Jezebel and her
prophets do not.[1]

Jezebel's home country! The Lord certainly has a sense of irony,
doesn't He? But what a perfect hiding place for Elijah. Ahab and
Jezebel would probably never have thought of looking in Jezebel's—
and Baal's—land for Yahweh's prophet. Nor would they have paid
much attention to a desperate widow—one of the most insignificant
faces among the crowd of her day.

With these overarching purposes in view, let's rejoin Elijah and
see what this experience was like from a human and emotional
perspective.

God's Command

Let's take a closer look at God's directives in verses 8–9. Verse 8
tells us: "Then the word of the Lord came to him, saying . . ." This
simple transition leads to a new chapter in the story. But three little
words, "came to him," also speak volumes about God's care for
Elijah. As the brook trickled away, it's possible that Elijah thought
God had lost track of him. But, of course, He had not, and God
reassured Elijah of this by coming to him rather than letting the
prophet search anxiously for Him.

Once the Lord came, He told Elijah,

> "Arise, go to Zarephath, which belongs to Sidon,
> and stay there; behold, I have commanded a widow
> there to provide for you." (v. 9)

Elijah didn't know what would happen after Cherith, just as we
don't know our futures either. But God does, and He makes sure
that we're provided for.

---

1. Paul R. House, *1, 2 Kings*, The New American Commentary Series (Nashville, Tenn.:
Broadman and Holman Publishers, 1995), vol. 8, pp. 214–15.

So far, Zarephath doesn't sound like much of a place for advanced training.[2] But consider whom God appointed to provide for Elijah: a widow. It probably would have been much easier for Elijah if God had commanded him to provide for the widow instead of the other way around. J. Robinson provides some insight into the particular widow Elijah would meet.

> Neither the woman nor her late husband seem to have had any family upon whom she could call for help. She was left alone to fend for herself and her son. Although she was a woman of some substance —she had a house and it was, or had been, prosperous enough to have a wooden room on the flat roof, the roof chamber as it is called—her plight was now desperate. She had no breadwinner and no status in the community so that she could be exploited and misused without hope of redress.[3]

Now Elijah—a strong, independent man who had stood before the king—must humble himself by allowing this bereaved, starving person to take care of him.

Elijah's Obedience

Having been given the go-ahead from God, Elijah set out for Zarephath (v. 10a). The long walk took him across wilderness, through Ahab's terrain, to a Gentile city on the Mediterranean coast of southern Sidon (16:31). All along the way, the pallor of drought settling deep into Israel's soil was his constant companion.

Finally he reached the gates of the city. How would he know which widow God had appointed him to meet? He would need to

---

2. Elijah's first place of training, Cherith, has the Hebrew root *karath*, which means "to cut off, cut down." At the brook, Elijah was cut off from other people and active service, as well as from harm. Interestingly, while Jezebel "destroyed" (literally, "cut off") Yahweh's prophets (1 Kings 18:4), Elijah was cut off from her murderous reach. The place of advanced training, Zarephath, meant "smelting place"—could it be that the Baal idols were smelted and manufactured here? The root word for Zarephath is *tsaraph*, meaning "to smelt, refine, test." It's also the root for "goldsmith," "silversmith," and "crucible." Even Elijah's faith would be refined by his experiences at Zarephath (compare 1 Pet. 1:6–7). See R. Laird Harris, Gleason L. Archer Jr., and Bruce K. Waltke, eds., *Theological Wordbook of the Old Testament* (Chicago, Ill.: Moody Press, 1980), vol. 2, pp. 777–78.

3. J. Robinson, *The First Book of Kings*, The Cambridge Bible Commentary Series (London, England: Cambridge University Press, 1972), p. 201.

give a little test to reveal the woman's openness to faith. So, when he saw a widow gathering some sticks nearby,

> he called to her and said, "Please get me a little water in a jar, that I may drink." As she was going to get it, he called to her and said, "Please bring me a piece of bread in your hand." But she said, "As the Lord your God lives, I have no bread, only a handful of flour in the bowl and a little oil in the jar; and behold, I am gathering a few sticks that I may go in and prepare for me and my son, that we may eat it and die." (17:10b–12)

Who would be providing for Elijah? Not just any widow, but a starving widow with a hungry boy to take care of . . . an impoverished widow preparing the last meal for herself and her son . . . a bereaved widow whose hope had died.

If we were in Elijah's place, we would probably be facing *the challenge of first impressions*. What would we have done—turn back to Cherith? Would the dry brook have looked more promising than this? Maybe we would have tried to find ourselves another hiding place. Perhaps we would have thought we found the wrong widow; surely God wouldn't have meant this one—this woman who was hardly capable of taking care of herself and her son!

Elijah, however, stayed where God told him to stay and proceeded to enter *the challenge of physical impossibility*.

The woman's eyes, understandably, were on the handful of flour in the bowl and the little bit of oil in the jar. It was physically impossible to keep two people, let alone three, alive on that scant amount of food. But Elijah's eyes were on the God who provides, and he wanted her to have the faith to put God first.

> Then Elijah said to her, "Do not fear; go, do as you have said, but make me a little bread cake from it first and bring it out to me, and afterward you may make one for yourself and for your son. For thus says the Lord God of Israel, 'The bowl of flour shall not be exhausted, nor shall the jar of oil be empty, until the day that the Lord sends rain on the face of the earth.'" (vv. 13–14)

How could Elijah say this? Because he *knew* from personal experience, not secondhand stories or academic theories, that God comes through when He says He will. How did the widow respond? With the faith Elijah was hoping to find:

> So she went and did according to the word of Elijah. (v. 15a)

God's Faithfulness

She was not disappointed.

> And she and he and her household ate for many days. The bowl of flour was not exhausted nor did the jar of oil become empty, according to the word of the Lord which He spoke through Elijah. (vv. 15b–16)

Granted, their menu would not make the favorite recipes section of *Bon Appétit* magazine—biscuits and water in the morning and water and biscuits in the evening—but their needs were miraculously met! As Paul R. House notes, "God's people have what they need and what Baal cannot provide."[4]

That widow met the true God in her kitchen! She looked into the bowl and found flour. She looked into the jar and found oil. Morning and evening, day in and day out, she witnessed God providing. She witnessed a God who cared for the poor and vulnerable. She witnessed a God whose power and blessing extended to all lands. She witnessed up-close the true prophet of the living God.[5] Without doubt, more than her body was nourished.

Lessons for Today

As we think about Elijah and the widow at Zarephath, let's linger over four lessons we can take with us when we enter a time of advanced training.

First: *God's leading is often surprising—don't analyze it.* If God tells you to go to Zarephath, then go—whether you can make sense out of it or not. If He leads you to stay, even though it may be very difficult, then stay; don't rack your brain trying to figure out His thinking. We are finite; God is infinite. He sees the whole picture, where we're only aware of fragmentary glimpses.

---

4. House, *1,2 Kings*, p. 215.

5. See Raymond B. Dillard's excellent insights into this story in his book *Faith in the Face of Apostasy: The Gospel according to Elijah and Elisha*, The Gospel according to the Old Testament Series (Phillipsburg, N.J.: Presbyterian and Reformed Publishing, 1999), pp. 23–27.

Second: *The beginning days are often the hardest—don't quit.* Wait out your first impressions. What if Elijah had given up when he first saw the desperateness of the widow? Everyone might have starved, and God would have been robbed of an opportunity to lovingly provide. Usually, the first days of a new situation are the hardest, but it won't be that tough the whole time. So bear with it.

Third: *God's promises often hinge on obedience—don't ignore your part.* Elijah was commanded to "arise, go, . . . and stay there" (v. 9). The widow was told to "go . . . make me a little bread cake from [the flour and oil] first" (v. 13). In each case, obedience preceded God's provision, so remember to do your part when God promises to provide for you.

Fourth: *God's provisions are often just enough—don't fail to thank Him.* Biscuits and water aren't exactly a smorgasbord of delights, but they filled hungry stomachs and sustained that household throughout a devastating drought. Have you thanked God for the ways He has met your needs? A grateful heart not only gives appreciation where it is due but also enriches the one who possesses it.

Living Insights

Elijah left Cherith knowing that God had "commanded a widow there to provide for" him (1 Kings 17:9). We can't help but wonder, though, if he was fully prepared for what he would see—a poor, starving woman who had given up hope and was ready to die. This wasn't the most promising first impression, was it?

Just about every member of the human race can identify with the challenge of first impressions. New schools, new jobs, new homes, new churches—all of them represent one of the toughest experiences life holds for us: beginnings. And most of us don't have a direct word from God to give us some idea of what to expect.

How well do you handle beginnings? In the space provided, write down one new situation you have encountered. It may range from tackling a new task at work to forming a new friendship, something big or something small.

_____

_____

_____

What was your first impression? What thoughts and feelings ran through your mind and heart?

_____

_____

_____

_____

_____

What effect did your first impression have on you? Did fear stop you from moving forward? Did you decide to go in a different direction? Or did you decide to wait and see beyond what your first impression told you?

_____

_____

_____

_____

_____

Elijah trusted God more than any first impression he may have had. That's something we can learn from, and so are the words of the philosopher Epictetus:

> Be not swept off your feet by the vividness of the
> impression, but say, "Impression, wait for me a little.
> Let me see what you are and what you represent.
> Let me try you."[6]

Or in the words of another wise man, "Trust in the Lord with all your heart, And do not lean on your own understanding" (Prov. 3:5). Sound advice, especially when it comes to first impressions.

6. Epictetus, as quoted in _Bartlett's Familiar Quotations_, 15th ed., rev. and enl., ed. Emily Morison Beck (Boston, Mass.: Little, Brown and Co., 1980), p. 121.

Questions for Group Discussion

1. In telling Elijah to go to Zarephath, the Lord was sending His witness to the heart of Baal country . . . and to the heart of a despairing widow and her son. Even in His grand spiritual scheme, God did not lose sight of a seemingly small detail like one hungry and hopeless woman. He often accomplishes great purposes through what can look like little means—ministering to human needs with love, care, and provision, for example. What are some other scriptural examples of this? Do you have any examples from your own life?

2. As we learned in our lesson, in order to receive the Lord's provision, we need to step out in faith and obey what He says. That's not always easy. The widow was staking her and her son's last meal on Elijah's promise. What risks have you had to take to receive what God was offering? What happened?

3. When the widow explained how little she had (1 Kings 17:12), what were the first three words Elijah spoke to her (v. 13a)? It's a gentle, encouraging response, isn't it? Elijah didn't shame her or rebuke her; he reassured her. What does his response teach you about how to nurture faith in others?

4. In a land stricken by drought, amidst a people who were struggling to find enough to eat, one widow took God at His word and received just what she needed. Has God ever provided for you this way? Not with literal oil and flour, but with encouragement, hope, security, or some other means in the midst of people who didn't believe God and lacked these things? What was your experience?

5. When God provides for you, how do you respond? Do you notice His provision, sense His care? Do you wish He'd given you more of what you wanted instead of just what you needed? Or do you humbly thank Him for what He has provided? A wise man once said, "Gratitude is the memory of the heart."[7] What are some ways you can more deeply cultivate gratitude in your heart?

7. Jean Baptiste Massieu, as quoted in *The Home Book of Quotations*, 10th ed., comp. Burton Stevenson (New York, N.Y.: Dodd, Mead and Co., 1967), p. 823.

Chapter 4

STANDING IN THE SHADOW OF GOD

1 Kings 17:17–24

"Great faith is not the faith that walks always in the light and knows no darkness, but the faith that perseveres in spite of God's seeming silences, and that faith will most certainly and surely get its reward." [1]

Scripture is replete with men and women who incarnated great faith, who modeled it in their generation and model it still today. For many of them, Hebrews 11 is their roll of honor—an encapsulation of both the darknesses they faced and the sure rewards they received. Consider some of their testimonies as their names ring out:

- "By faith Noah, being warned by God about things not yet seen, in reverence prepared an ark for the salvation of his household" (v. 7a).

- "By faith Abraham, when he was called, obeyed by going out to a place which he was to receive for an inheritance; and he went out, not knowing where he was going" (v. 8).

- "By faith even Sarah herself received ability to conceive, even beyond the proper time of life" (v. 11a).

- "By faith Joseph, when he was dying, made mention of the exodus of the sons of Israel, and gave orders concerning his bones" (v. 22).

- "By faith Moses, when he had grown up, refused to be called the son of Pharaoh's daughter, . . . considering the reproach of Christ greater riches than the treasures of Egypt" (vv. 24, 26).

Out of breath from this roll call of faith, the inspired chronicler then asks, "And what more shall I say?" (v. 32a). For time would indeed fail us if every person and act of faith were listed, from David

---

1. Father Andrew, as quoted in *The Harper Religious and Inspirational Quotation Companion*, comp. Margaret Pepper (New York, N.Y.: Harper and Row, Publishers, 1989), p. 172.

to the prophets, from the shutting of lions' mouths to women receiving back their dead by resurrection (vv. 32b–35a).[2]

One more person of great faith needs to be listed, however, and that's Elijah. His faith would pass through a crucible at Zarephath— here he would have to trust God to do something never before recorded: raise someone from the dead. And it's not just any someone, but the son of the impoverished widow he had been boarding with.

Context and Atmosphere

Our story opens with the words, "Now it came about after these things" (1 Kings 17:17a). What things? Most recently, Elijah's meeting the widow whom God had appointed and the Lord's compassionately providing relief for her, her son, and Elijah himself. Our immediate context, then, is the widow's home in Zarephath, where the Lord's prophet remained safely hidden from Ahab and Jezebel (vv. 8–16).

The greater spiritual context, though, is God's ongoing campaign against Baal. With the drought, the Lord had shown who truly controls the weather and the fertility of the crops. With the brook and ravens of Cherith, the Lord had shown who truly commands nature. With the flour and oil of Zarephath, the Lord had shown who truly sustains life. Now, with the death and restoration of the widow's son, the Lord would show who truly has the power not only to sustain life but to *give* it. Baal was only a deluding mirage; Yahweh is the one true God, the sovereign Lord who has the power of life in His very self.

With this spiritual context in mind, let's see how God works out His plan at the human level, where the widow and Elijah were grieved and confused by the sudden death of her young son.

Sickness and Death

Safe, fed, maybe even enjoying the taste of family life, Elijah was suddenly jolted out of Zarephath's comfortable routine by a grievous event:

Now it came about after these things that the

---

2. *Resurrection*, in this context, refers to a resuscitation of life. This occurs when a person comes back to life with the same body. *Resurrection*, technically, refers to a new life with a new body. See Charles C. Ryrie, *Basic Theology* (Wheaton, Ill.: Scripture Press Publications, Victor Books, 1986), pp. 517–22.

son of the woman, the mistress of the house, became sick; and his sickness was so severe that there was no breath left in him. (v. 17)

The Hebrew word for *breath* here, *neshamah*, is the same word used in Genesis 2:7, where the Lord created Adam and "breathed into his nostrils the breath of life." So 1 Kings 17:17 is not describing a respiratory ailment; it is telling us that the boy was no longer breathing. It is telling us that the only family, the only loved one the widow had left, had died.

Who can fathom the agony of losing a child?

> Of all deaths, that of a child is most unnatural and hardest to bear.
>
> In Carl Jung's words, it is "a period placed before the end of the sentence," sometimes when the sentence has hardly begun.
>
> We expect the old to die. The separation is always difficult, but it comes as no surprise.
>
> But the child, the youth? Life lies ahead, with its beauty, its wonder, its potential. Death is a cruel thief when it strikes down the young.[3]

The widow, already bereft of her husband, now reeled with this fresh loss. Her future, her plans, her dreams—all embodied in her young son—lay spent and lifeless in her desperate arms. In her anguish and rage at this cruel thief, she struck out at the only person near to her: Elijah.

> "What do I have to do with you, O man of God? You have come to me to bring my iniquity to remembrance and to put my son to death!" (v. 18)

Into her shattered heart a dark intruder came . . . guilt. We've no idea what her "iniquity" was, but in her mind it was enough to merit divine, merciless punishment. So Elijah, the humble man of God, became in her mind Elijah, God's emissary of judgment.

---

3. Joseph Bayly, *The Last Thing We Talk About*, rev. ed. (Elgin, Ill.: David C. Cook Publishing Co., 1973), p. 65. The author lost three sons: one at eighteen days, after surgery; another at five years, from leukemia; and the third at eighteen years, after a sledding accident complicated by mild hemophilia (p. 66).

Before this God of judgment, the widow felt utterly, hopelessly condemned.[4]

Faith and Prayer

Looking at her tear-streaked face and eyes frantic with grief, Elijah saw beyond her anger and was moved with compassion. Rather than arguing with her or defending himself, he stood with her, bearing the weight of her pain in a gentle, eloquent silence—a silence that would be broken only by simple words of faith.

> He said to her, "Give me your son." Then he took him from her bosom and carried him up to the upper room where he was living, and laid him on his own bed. (v. 19)

As the widow had cradled her boy in her arms, so Elijah now cradled her heart in his. He got alone with God in a protected place where he could pour out his heart and search God's mercy. And he took the risk of getting deeply, personally involved in her need.

> He called to the Lord and said, "O Lord my God, have you also brought calamity to the widow with whom I am staying, by causing her son to die?" Then he stretched himself upon the child three times, and called to the Lord, and said, "O Lord my God, I pray You, let this child's life return to him." (vv. 20–21)

Once . . . twice . . . three times Elijah stretched himself upon the boy—body to body, arm to arm, leg to leg. It was as if Elijah somehow thought that a transfusion of life could occur under this canopy of contact. But Elijah was stretched in more than body; his faith strained for a miracle never before performed, reached for a mercy God had never before bestowed.

And God grasped His servant's outstretched hand.

---

4. Commentator Simon J. DeVries asks, "What sins, and how does sickness bring them to remembrance? Her sins must remain her own secret, but her theology of divine judgment is so erroneous that Elijah must act to refute it. . . . If words could be borrowed from the NT, the purpose of this lad's sore sickness would rather be 'that the works of God might be made manifest in him' (John 9:3)." *Word Biblical Commentary: 1 Kings* (Waco, Tex.: Word Books, Publisher, 1985), vol. 12, p. 221. As the book of Job attests, the sorrows of our lives are not always a result of our sins.

Miracle and Praise

Sweat beading on his forehead, Elijah held his breath and watched the boy intently. Were those his eyelids fluttering? Did his finger really twitch? Oh, how gracious and kind the Lord is!

> The Lord heard the voice of Elijah, and the life of the child returned to him and he revived.[5] (v. 22)

Panting, laughing, praising God, Elijah helped the boy sit up. The boy's small, pallid face brightened with a sunrise glow. His listless eyes danced with the light of life again. And Elijah's heart filled with grateful joy—a joy he could hardly wait to give to a certain mother:

> Elijah took the child and brought him down from the upper room into the house and gave him to his mother; and Elijah said, "See, your son is alive." (v. 23)

No "Ta da!" No "I told you I was a man of God." No "Look what I have done!" Just a tender "See, your son is alive." See, God is alive, powerful, caring, and kind. See, He, not Baal, is the one and only true God. And as her burning tears of sorrow ebbed, her eyes cleared . . . and she saw:

> Then the woman said to Elijah, "Now I know that you are a man of God and that the word of the Lord in your mouth is truth." (v. 24)

As Simon J. DeVries notes, "The woman has called Elijah 'man of God' out of reverence and respect, but now she knows him to be a 'man of God' whose word from God is truth."[6] Interestingly, Elijah had been "verified as an authentic man of God and the bearer of God's word by a daughter of the very people he opposed"[7]— Jezebel's people.

---

5. J. Robinson, looking at the bigger spiritual picture, poses the idea that this story was included in 1 Kings to show Elijah's prophetic vocation as the calling "to breathe new life into God's child, Israel, who was fast becoming spiritually lifeless." *The First Book of Kings*, The Cambridge Bible Commentary Series (London, England: Cambridge University Press, 1972), p. 203.

6. DeVries, *Word Biblical Commentary: 1 Kings*, p. 222.

7. Gene Rice, *Nations under God: A Commentary on the Book of 1 Kings*, International Theological Commentary Series (Grand Rapids, Mich.: William B. Eerdmans Publishing Co., 1990) p. 145.

Concluding Applications

"Now I know that you are a man of God," the widow said, because she saw Elijah's faith and the power of God working through him. Can we be like Elijah? Most likely not in the prophetic and miraculous sense, but we can be people of great faith. Let's examine how Elijah demonstrated his faith through four of his inner attitudes.

First, *he demonstrated calmness and contentment.* This may seem trivial, but not a word of complaint fell from his lips about his accommodations or his food. He trusted God's wisdom in how the Lord chose to provide for him, and he was grateful for God's care. Are we? Often, our food and shelter are items that generally agitate us if they are not just right. Faith is cultivated in a grateful spirit that knows God has given enough.

Second, *he demonstrated gentleness and self-control.* When the widow lashed out at Elijah in her searing grief, he remained silent until he knew what to do. Then, gently, he lifted her burden from her and took it for his own, presenting the concern to God.

Third, *he demonstrated undiminished faith.* Elijah stretched himself out in prayer again and again until he received an answer. Had God said no, he would have known and stopped; but he felt the Lord's Spirit heavy upon him to intercede for the boy. Such sensitivity to the Lord comes from an intimate knowledge of God and is learned by trusting Him through many Cherith and Zarephath experiences.

Fourth, *he demonstrated humility.* When God displayed His power, Elijah gave Him center stage. He stood in the wings and listened to the applause that was not for him, but for God's merciful and mighty work. Elijah's humility came from realizing that he had been allowed to be a part of something beyond himself, beyond what he could have ever dreamed.

All over this world, there are "widows"—the broken, the needy, the hurting—who are hungry and crying out for God's presence. They don't need indignant arguing or defensive declarations against the questions that spring from their anguish; they just need to feel the touch of God's care. So—in gentleness and humility, in seeking God and opening our hearts to involvement—this is where great faith is demonstrated. This is how we can be like Elijah.

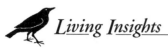 *Living Insights*

"What do I have to do with you, O man of God? You have come to me *to bring my iniquity to remembrance* and to put my son to death!" (1 Kings 17:18, emphasis added)

Between the lines of the widow's words are the haunting thoughts, *It's my fault! I'm a bad person, and God has no mercy. He's punishing me for past sins.* These were cruel, crippling thoughts that only drove her anguish deeper. What's worse, these feelings weren't telling her the truth.

Can any of us really say with certainty what God is doing in a tragic situation? Are *we* always the cause of what's going on around us? Or is this merely the acidic lie of shame, disfiguring our hearts with unreasonable guilt?

Can you identify with the widow of Zarephath? Do you struggle with condemning feelings when tragedy strikes you? What kind of thoughts and accusations sear your spirit?

_____

_____

_____

_____

Do you fear that God is against you in such times? Do you convince yourself that everyone but you is eligible for His love and forgiveness? Try to articulate what you often feel.

_____

_____

_____

_____

Hard times are hard enough without shame's insidious attacks. To protect yourself against its lies, you need to have a clear understanding of God's heart. He is so very ready and willing to respond to your cry for forgiveness and cleansing. And once He has forgiven,

He never brings it up again. Only Satan, the accuser, does that.[8]

Take some time to learn more about God's heart through the following verses.

Psalm 51:17 _____

_____

Psalm 103:8–14 _____

_____

_____

_____

_____

_____

Isaiah 57:15–19 _____

_____

_____

_____

_____

_____

Romans 8:1, 33–34 _____

_____

_____

_____

According to 1 John 1:9, when we confess our sins to the Lord, "He is faithful and righteous"—true to His Word—"to forgive us our sins and to cleanse us from all unrighteousness." So when painful circumstances come your way, bringing with them the specters of past sins, remember that you are forgiven . . . and let Christ open the door.

---

8. The Hebrew word for *accuser* is *satan.*

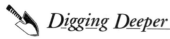 *Digging Deeper*

What do you say to someone who is grieving? It is a difficult question because there are no formulas, no "if such-and-such happens, use response A; if this or that occurs, use response B."

Nicholas Wolterstorff, who lost his twenty-five-year-old son in a climbing accident, reflects:

> Some people are gifted with words of wisdom. For such, one is profoundly grateful. . . . But not all are gifted in that way.[9]

Elijah, perhaps, was one of those who are not gifted that way. So he kept still . . . he kept the widow safe from any further hurt that could have been inflicted by untimely words. And perhaps the widow heard the unspoken words of his heart—why else would she have let him take her son?

> The heart that speaks is heard more than the words spoken. And if you can't think of anything at all to say, just say, "I can't think of anything to say. But I want you to know that we are with you in your grief."[10]

"I am with you in your grief," Elijah's heart seemed to say. He didn't turn away or promise not to intrude on her privacy. He came close, took her burden out of her arms and into his, and joined her before God in her suffering.

He did what Wolterstorff longed for.

> If you think your task as comforter is to tell me that really, all things considered, it's not so bad, you do not sit with me in my grief but place yourself off in the distance away from me. Over there, you are of no help. What I need to hear from you is that you recognize how painful it is. I need to hear from you that you are with me in my desperation. To comfort

9. Nicholas Wolterstorff, *Lament for a Son* (Grand Rapids, Mich.: William B. Eerdmans Publishing Co., 1987), p. 34.

10. Wolterstorff, *Lament for a Son*, p. 34.

me, you have to come close. Come sit beside me on
my mourning bench.[11]

Close and quiet—but not stoic. Elijah did not sit stiffly on the widow's mourning bench; he stretched himself over her pain three times, calling out to God all the while. As Wolterstorff observes, "Your tears are salve on our wound."[12]

Drawing near to someone in the intensity of grief is not easy, but it's the only way to put salve on their wound. Hopefully, Elijah's example and Wolterstorff's words will give you a start in learning what you can do to help those who grieve. To help you further, devote some time to these resources.

- Learn about the grieving process. See Joseph Bayly, *The Last Thing We Talk About* (Elgin, Ill.: David C. Cook Publishing Co., 1973); Paula D'Arcy, *When Your Friend Is Grieving: Building a Bridge of Love* (Wheaton, Ill.: Harold Shaw Publishers, 1990); Bernadine Kreis and Alice Pattie, *Up from Grief: Patterns of Recovery* (San Francisco, Calif.: Harper and Row, Publishers, 1969).

- Read about how grief and sorrow feel so that you can better understand your suffering friend's feelings. See Nicholas Wolterstorff, *Lament for a Son* (Grand Rapids, Mich.: William B. Eerdmans Publishing Co., 1987); C. S. Lewis, *A Grief Observed* (San Francisco, Calif.: Harper and Row, Publishers, 1961); and any other book describing personal experience with grief.

- Get some instruction on how to comfort. For starters, read Warren W. and David W. Wiersbe, *Comforting the Bereaved* (Chicago, Ill.: Moody Press, 1985); and Katie Maxwell, *Bedside Manners* (Grand Rapids, Mich.: Baker Book House, 1990).

- Study how Christ responded to grief by meditating on John 11.

And remember, unlike this widow's experience, most grief doesn't end in a day, as Wolterstorff confesses:

And later, when you ask me how I am doing and
I respond with a quick, thoughtless "Fine" or "OK,"
stop me sometime and ask, "No, I mean *really.*"[13]

---

11. Wolterstorff, *Lament for a Son,* p. 34.

12. Wolterstorff, *Lament for a Son,* p. 35.

13. Wolterstorff, *Lament for a Son,* p. 35.

Questions for Group Discussion

1. The Lord had told Elijah to live with a widow in Zarephath; He had promised that the widow's supply of flour and oil would not run out; and Elijah, the widow, and her son had been nourished by the God-given bread. All was going well, when, without warning, death blindsided the household—the widow's young son died suddenly. What a shock! Do you think Elijah was shaken by this experience? Why or why not? What can you tell from what he said—and didn't say—in this story?

2. Even God's own prophet couldn't completely know the infinite mind of the Lord. Elijah couldn't explain why the boy died, and he didn't try to. Do you sometimes feel that because you're a Christian, you should be able to explain why tragedies happen—why God lets "bad things happen to good people"? What does Elijah's response teach you? How can it help you deal differently with hurting people?

3. Elijah had learned how to pronounce tough judgments (v. 1) and how to provide encouragement and blessing (vv. 13–14). But when the widow's son died, he learned an even more precious lesson: how to intercede. He learned to take into his own heart another's pain and bring it to God. Why is it so essential for a person of God to have an interceding heart?

4. What do you think God might have been teaching Elijah and the widow in this story? Why is it so important to God that we know He has the power of life and death and that His words are true?

Chapter 5

THE GOD WHO
ANSWERS BY FIRE

1 Kings 18:1–40

After more than three years, Elijah's time of hiding finally came to an end. The Lord gave him these new instructions:

> "Go, show yourself to Ahab, and I will send rain on
> the face of the earth." (1 Kings 18:1)

Rain! How long it had been since Elijah felt the cool, watery drops run down his face and hair and hands. Finally, the suffering earth would be refreshed, and the starving people would soon have their fill. Relief was on its way—but not before it had been shown with absolute, indisputable clarity who had withheld it and who would give it: Yahweh, not Baal.

So Elijah said good-bye to the widow and her son and "went to show himself to Ahab" (v. 2a). Let's join him on his journey— a journey that will take us to the heights of Mount Carmel and the victory that will leave no doubt about who the real God is.

Return to Israel

How had Israel fared during the drought? Not too well. The writer of 1 Kings reported that "the famine was severe in Samaria" (v. 2b). Samaria was Ahab's region—his father had established Israel's capital there (16:24)—and it appears that the Lord especially targeted Ahab and Jezebel with the misery of drought and famine. Ahab and his trusted servant, Obadiah, were forced to search throughout the region to find whatever water and vegetation might be left for the king's horses, mules, and cattle (vv. 5–6).

On the spiritual front, things hadn't been much better during the drought. Jezebel had initiated a slaughter of the Lord's prophets, but Obadiah had secretly hidden and cared for a hundred of them (18:4). Obadiah was in a tough spot: he was a trusted servant of a wicked king, yet he "feared the Lord greatly" (v. 3). The writer of 1 Kings subtly expressed Obadiah's tension in the search for grass and water for Ahab's animals: "Ahab went one way . . . and Obadiah went another way" (v. 6). Little did Obadiah know that his way would lead him to Elijah!

Elijah and Obadiah

Hardly able to believe his eyes, Obadiah lay prostrate before Elijah and asked, "Is this you, Elijah my master?" (v. 7). Elijah assured him it was and told him, "Go, say to your master, 'Behold, Elijah is here'" (v. 8). At this, Obadiah panicked. Practically babbling, he told Elijah that the king had looked everywhere for him— Ahab had made whole nations "swear that they could not find you" (v. 10). So should he now tell the king he'd found Elijah, only to have the Spirit snatch the prophet out of reach again (v. 12)? *Ahab will kill me!* the frightened Obadiah repeated three times (vv. 9, 12, 14). In essence, he asked Elijah, "Haven't I feared the Lord since I was a child and even risked my life to protect His prophets? What have I done that you want Ahab to kill me?" (vv. 13–14).

Calmly but firmly, Elijah replied:

> "As the Lord of hosts[1] lives, before whom I stand, I
> will surely show myself to him today." (v. 15)

With this assurance, Obadiah left to give Elijah's message to Ahab. And the king went immediately to see the prophet (v. 16).

Elijah and Ahab

What would happen when "the representative of institutional power —the baalizing king" would meet "the representative of spiritual power—the humble, spirit-filled prophet"?[2] It wouldn't be pleasant, as you can imagine. Ahab arrogantly dodged his role in the drought and tried to put the blame on Elijah: "Is this you, you troubler of Israel?" (v. 17). But Elijah wouldn't let him wriggle away from the truth:

> "I have not troubled Israel, but you and your father's

---

1. "The Lord of hosts" is a name for God that highlights His power and might. This "was the title by which Yahweh had especially been known in the days of the old tribal league. It was then the rallying cry of the tribes for battle. . . . All that Israel had come to learn of the character of the God she served was expressed by that title. LORD of Hosts expressed therefore the character and demands of Yahweh the God of Israel, and embodied the emotional force of the loyalty which Israel felt to her own history, tradition and forefathers." J. Robinson, *The First Book of Kings,* The Cambridge Bible Commentary Series (London, England: Cambridge University Press, 1972), p. 206.

2. Simon J. DeVries, *Word Biblical Commentary: 1 Kings* (Waco, Tex.: Word Books, Publisher, 1985), vol. 12, p. 219.

house have, because you have forsaken the commandments of the Lord and you have followed the Baals."
(v. 18)

Without giving Ahab a chance to reply, Elijah instead gave
orders to the king:

> "Now then send and gather to me all Israel at Mount
> Carmel, together with 450 prophets of Baal and 400
> prophets of the Asherah, who eat at Jezebel's table."
> (v. 19)

Probably surprised and pleased that Elijah would propose a plan
that would leave him outnumbered, Ahab agreed and summoned
everyone to Mount Carmel (v. 20).

Confrontation on Carmel

With the prophets and people in place, Elijah issued a challenge
of decision:

> "How long will you hesitate[3] between two opinions?
> If the Lord is God, follow Him; but if Baal, follow
> him." But the people did not answer him a word.
> (v. 21)

No answer. To choose Yahweh meant rejecting Ahab and Jezebel's god—and that meant persecution. And, after all, Baal wasn't
so bad, was he? Before the drought, the economy had been strong;
why ruin a good thing? Couldn't they pay homage to both the Lord
and Baal—keep everybody happy? So the people said nothing. But
Elijah would not let them keep sitting on that fence.

> Then Elijah said to the people, "I alone am left a
> prophet of the Lord, but Baal's prophets are 450
> men. Now let them give us two oxen; and let them
> choose one ox for themselves and cut it up, and place

---

3. The Hebrew word for *hesitate* is *pasach*, meaning "to limp." In the Israelites' indecision,
they were trying to hobble after both Yahweh and Baal, but the Lord and the idol took them
in opposite directions. The writer may also have made a play on words in this passage—the
word *leaped* in verse 26, describing Baal's prophets' dance around their altar, is the same
word *pasach*. "In her religious ambivalence Israel is but engaging in a wild and futile religious
'dance.'" J. Robert Vannoy, note on 1 Kings 18:21, in *The NIV Study Bible*, gen. ed. Kenneth
L. Barker (Grand Rapids, Mich.: Zondervan Bible Publishers, 1985), p. 511.

it on the wood, but put no fire under it; and I will prepare the other ox and lay it on the wood, and I will not put a fire under it. Then you call on the name of your god, and I will call on the name of the Lord, and the God who answers by fire, He is God." And all the people said, "That is a good idea." (vv. 22–24)

If the people wouldn't answer, God would. And a decision would have to be made.

"O Baal, Answer Us"

Elijah gave the prophets of Baal first pick of the oxen and the chance to go first. "But put no fire under it," he reminded them (v. 25). From morning until noon, they called to their god, "O Baal, answer us."

But no one answered.

So they intensified their plea, adding a limping altar dance to their cries (v. 26). Still there was no fire, but Elijah turned up the heat:

> It came about at noon, that Elijah mocked them and said, "Call out with a loud voice, for he is a god; either he is occupied or gone aside,[4] or is on a journey, or perhaps he is asleep and needs to be awakened." (v. 27)

That really got them going: "They cried with a loud voice and cut themselves according to their custom with swords and lances until the blood gushed out on them" (v. 28). Then they raved until the time of the evening sacrifice (v. 29a).

> But there was no voice, no one answered, and no one paid attention. (v. 29b)

"Answer Me, O Lord"

Having seen enough of this pathetic nonsense, Elijah called the

---

4. The phrase "gone aside" has been "taken by some as a euphemism for going to the toilet. . . . 'Elijah's satire in a nut-shell is the raciest comment ever made on Pagan mythology' (James A. Montgomery, *The Book of Kings*, 302)." Gene Rice, *Nations under God: A Commentary on the Book of 1 Kings*, International Theological Commentary Series (Grand Rapids, Mich.: William B. Eerdmans Publishing Co., 1990), p. 151.

people to him. They watched him rebuild the altar of the Lord, which Jezebel most likely had torn down. He took twelve stones to represent all the tribes—not just the ten of the northern kingdom—and to remind them where they came from: the twelve sons of their patriarch Jacob, whom the Lord had renamed Israel (vv. 30–31). With the altar repaired, Elijah did something curious: he dug a trench around the altar (v. 32). Then, when he had arranged the wood and the ox on it, he told the people,

> "Fill four pitchers with water and pour it on the burnt offering and on the wood." And he said, "Do it a second time," and they did it a second time. And he said, "Do it a third time," and they did it a third time. The water flowed around the altar and he also filled the trench with water. (vv. 33–35)

You can't light a fire with wet wood—what was Elijah thinking? He was thinking that the Lord Almighty could do anything, and he prayed that the people would see and believe too.

> "O Lord, the God of Abraham, Isaac and Israel, today let it be known that You are God in Israel and that I am Your servant and I have done all these things at Your word. Answer me, O Lord, answer me, that this people may know that You, O Lord, are God, and that You have turned their heart back again." (vv. 36–37)

Would the Lord answer? They didn't have long to wait:

> Then the fire of the Lord fell and consumed the burnt offering and the wood and the stones and the dust, and licked up the water that was in the trench. (v. 38)

The offering, the wood, the stones—even the dust—all turned to ash in an instant! The Lord heard and answered His prophet, with no waiting, frantic dancing, shouting, or bloodletting required.

Finally, the people stopped limping between two opinions and gave their answer:

> When all the people saw it, they fell on their faces; and they said, "The Lord, He is God; the Lord, He is God." (v. 39)

Baal was a myth, and his prophets had intimidated the people into lies and degradation. So Elijah told the people to seize those prophets, and he killed them at the brook Kishon, removing a malignancy that had threatened the spiritual life of Israel (see Deut. 13:1–5).

Lessons from the Mountain

From this story, it is crystal clear that the Lord really cares whether our hearts are wholly His. As you seek to walk with God and give Him more and more of your heart, take these lessons with you for guidance and encouragement along the way.

First, *divided allegiance is as wrong as open idolatry.* The easiest thing to do when outnumbered is to assume a mediocre stance of noncommitment. But if you try to straddle a religious fence, as the Israelites did, you court the danger of falling off on the wrong side. Elijah confronted religious apostasy, prodding the people to make a decision and get off that fence.

Second, *our most effective tool is prayer.* In contrast with Baal's prophets, Elijah simply prayed. He didn't do anything flashy; he didn't draw attention to himself; he didn't try to take on the false prophets in his own power. He just prayed that God would affirm what he had been telling the people so they would know the Lord wanted them back. Prayer does not manipulate God into doing what we want. Rather, it expresses our willingness to conform the desires of our hearts to the desires of His. Prayer invites God to work so that others might see that He is real and turn to Him.

And last, *never underestimate the power of one life totally dedicated to the Lord.* Those 850 prophets of Baal and Asherah were no match for Elijah because his life was wholly devoted to the Lord's service. God works, even through frail people like us, when our hearts are completely His.

Elijah's faith encourages us to live in a way that reveals to others the reality of God. Our task is to help them comprehend God's truth and feel His love so much that they, too, turn their hearts to Him.

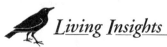 *Living Insights*

How could Elijah stand so fearlessly before King Ahab, nearly a thousand false prophets, and a nation of "no comment" fence-sitters? Perhaps we can find a clue in one of the names he used for God: the Lord of Hosts.[5] Let's spend some time digging into the meaning of this name to see how knowing God this way can strengthen our faith.

Scholars tell us that Lord of Hosts means:

- We have help in God, especially when we have no other help;
- God's help is ever near;
- God disciplines His people and restores them to Himself;
- He strikes down His people's adversaries and delivers His own;
- He has all the forces of heaven at His disposal to accomplish His will;
- He is more powerful than any earthly army or kingdom and any cosmic force;
- He is the most exalted king and ruler;
- Through His power He created the mountains, seas, and winds, and He controls all nature;[6]
- "He is master over every force."[7]

Is God "master over every force" in your life? Do you acknowledge His rule over your choices and commitments? In what ways does your life reflect the reality of God's being Lord of Hosts? Do you find reassurance in His power, for instance, or have you experienced His help?

---

5. The New International Version renders this title as "Lord Almighty."

6. See Andrew Jukes, *The Names of God: Discovering God as He Desires to be Known* (Grand Rapids, Mich.: Kregel Publications, 1967), pp. 157, 160, 161–62, 171; and R. Laird Harris, Gleason L. Archer Jr., and Bruce K. Waltke, eds., *Theological Wordbook of the Old Testament* (Chicago, Ill.: Moody Press, 1980), vol. 2, pp. 750–51.

7. Harris, Archer, and Waltke, *Theological Wordbook of the Old Testament*, p. 751.

In what areas of your life are you not acknowledging Him as Lord of Hosts? For example, are there some fearful situations that seem beyond His help? Or are you fighting Him for control of certain areas of your life? Or does He seem distant, not too concerned about what happens to you?

_____

_____

_____

_____

In order to get to know Him more as Lord of Hosts, invest some prayerful time in the following verses. Write down the characteristics and values that are associated with this particular name. Ask the Lord to make you more sensitive to this aspect of Himself and to help you find in Him the strength and support you need.

1 Samuel 17:45	Jeremiah 11:20
Isaiah 2:12	Jeremiah 31:35
Isaiah 5:16	Jeremiah 50:34
Isaiah 6:3	Zechariah 7:9–10
Isaiah 37:16	

_____

_____

_____

_____

_____

_____

_____

_____

_____

_____

_____

_____

Questions for Group Discussion

1. Some of the people in Elijah's day probably deserted the Lord to serve Baal. But some may have tried to combine both religions, paying respect to the old way but wanting to keep up with the times. Have you felt that tension between your ancient Christian faith and the pull of your modern culture? In what areas is the tension most challenging to you? Why?

2. How have you handled the demands of your faith and the pressures of your culture? Have you sometimes been tempted to desert some of God's ways to fit in better? Or have you taken the "embrace the best of both worlds" approach? What has been the result?

3. Robert Louis Stevenson once wrote, "The cruellest lies are often told in silence. A man may have sat in a room for hours and not opened his mouth, and yet come out of that room a disloyal friend."[8] The Israelites' silence to Elijah's challenge in 1 Kings 18:21 underscored their disloyalty to Yahweh. Have you ever remained silent when you should have spoken up for God? What was the situation? Why did you choose to keep quiet?

4. What do you learn about God in the contrast between His response to Elijah and Baal's response to his prophets? (See especially v. 29.)

5. What is the most significant thing you've learned from this story?

8. Robert Louis Stevenson, as quoted in *The Columbia Dictionary of Quotations*, licensed from Columbia University Press. Copyright © 1993, 1995 by Columbia University Press. All rights reserved. As used on Microsoft Bookshelf 98, © & ℗ 1987–1996 Microsoft Corporation. All rights reserved.

Chapter 6

A MAN OF GOD . . .
A PROMISE OF GOD

1 Kings 18:41–46

On Mount Carmel, the people of Israel saw and felt the heat of God's fire—an image of God's holy character since the days of Mount Sinai, when Israel witnessed the mountain ablaze with the presence of God. Before they crossed over to the Promised Land, Moses had warned them, "For the Lord your God is a consuming fire, a jealous God" (Deut. 4:24). And he urged them to respond to what they had witnessed:

> "Know therefore today, and take it to your heart,
> that the Lord, He is God in heaven above and on
> the earth below; there is no other." (v. 39)

So when the Lord's fire consumed Elijah's sacrifice and the very altar stones themselves, the prophet didn't need to tell the people how to respond. They instinctively fell on their faces before Yahweh: "The Lord, He is God; the Lord, He is God" (1 Kings 18:39).

Israel's repentance signaled the end of God's three-year judgment on the land. Soon the drought of God's discipline would be over, and the showers of His blessings would refresh Israel once again. For rain was soon to come, just as the Lord had promised (18:1).

God's Promise to His People: Review

Like fire, the image of rain also had deep roots in the history of the Hebrew people. When the Lord prepared the Israelites to enter Canaan, He told them that this land would be different from the land they had known for centuries. In Egypt, crops were irrigated by the Nile River, but the rocky hills and steep valleys of Canaan would need to drink "the rain of heaven" to be fruitful (Deut. 11:10–12).

The Lord's promise was not unconditional, however; the key to keeping the rain coming season after season was the condition of the people's hearts. Moses told them:

> "It shall come about, if you listen obediently to my
> commandments which I am commanding you today,

to love the Lord your God and to serve Him with all your heart and all your soul, that He will give the rain for your land in its season, the early and late rain, that you may gather in your grain and your new wine and your oil. He will give grass in your fields for your cattle, and you will eat and be satisfied." (vv. 13–15)

The gracious hand of Yahweh released the spring and winter rains . . . not the capricious hand of Baal. Now that the people had relearned this truth and renewed their ancient pledge to serve the Lord only (see Exod. 24:3–8; 1 Kings 18:39), the Lord would fulfill His promise to send "the rain of heaven," just as He said He would.

God's Promise to Elijah: Exposition

In addition to keeping His promise to the nation, the Lord would also keep the promise He had personally made to Elijah.

The Promise Declared

Remember God's word to His prophet at the beginning of 1 Kings 18? The Lord came to Zarephath, about three years after He'd given Elijah the message of drought, and gave him these new directions:

"Go, show yourself to Ahab, and I will send rain on the face of the earth." (v. 1)

Notice, even for Elijah the promise of rain was conditioned on obedience. He first had to show himself to Ahab, and then the Lord would bring rain to satisfy the parched soil's thirst.

And, as we saw in our previous chapter, Elijah obeyed without hesitation. He confronted Ahab and all the false prophets with a direct challenge backed by fervent prayer. Then, in one blinding moment, fire fell from heaven and consumed the entire altar—and all the people knew who the real God was (vv. 16–39). Elijah had finished his part, the people had repented, and now it was time for rain.

Elijah's next words to the stunned and spiritually defeated Ahab revealed the prophet's unwavering trust in God:

Now Elijah said to Ahab, "Go up, eat and drink; for there is the sound of the roar of a heavy shower." (v. 41)

Elijah's confidence in Yahweh was so great that he told Ahab the famine was over and the feast could begin—before even one drop of rain had fallen. How could Elijah be so certain? Because God always keeps His word, and the prophet heard the sound of the promised rain with "the ear of faith."[1] His heart and mind were flooded with rain, though the skies across the horizon, as far as he could see, were cloudless.

The Promise Claimed

With Ahab eating and drinking his fill, Elijah ascended the region's sentinel, Mount Carmel, to come before the Lord again in prayer (v. 42). As the story unfolds, we can learn five things about prayer from Elijah's actions during this mountaintop moment of faith.

First: *Elijah separated himself.* On the peak of Mount Carmel, he found an isolated place to devote himself to prayer and to watch God's hand at work.

Second: *Elijah humbled himself.* The latter half of verse 42 notes that "he crouched down on the earth and put his face between his knees." This posture showed that Elijah didn't approach his Lord arrogantly but with sincerity and utter humility. And it underscored that he didn't take credit for routing Jezebel's hundreds of religious advisors. Since he stood alone, humanly speaking, against the king and the false prophets, he could have become proud of his courage and victory. But instead, he dropped his head between his knees and was humble before the true Victor.

Third: *Elijah was confident and specific.* We often think that prayer is only the time when our heads are bowed before the Lord. Yet as we watch Elijah, we learn from his words to his servant that it includes an active waiting for God's response: "Go up now, look toward the sea," Elijah urged him (v. 43a).

Elijah had prayed so specifically and so confidently for God to fulfill His promise of rain that he had no doubt his servant would see storm clouds gathering on the horizon. The people had abandoned Baal and returned to their Lord, and now Elijah was absolutely certain that God would lift the covenant curse for their prior unfaithfulness.

Fourth: *Elijah was persistent and fervent.* With his servant's eyes

---

1. Gene Rice, *Nations under God: A Commentary on the Book of 1 Kings,* International Theological Commentary Series (Grand Rapids, Mich.: William B. Eerdmans Publishing Co., 1990), p. 154.

trained on the sea, Elijah waited for a sign of rain. But his servant only said,

> "There is nothing." And [Elijah] said, "Go back"
> seven times. (v. 43b)

Nothing. Some prayer warriors may sink in a mire of doubt with that word, but not this man of God. For the widow's son, Elijah prayed three times before seeing signs of life. Here he prayed and sent his helper not just three times, but four, five, six, *seven* times. And he probably would have kept at it for as long as it took to see God act.

Elijah tenaciously hung on to God's promise in fervent prayer. Commentator Ronald Wallace gives us an insight into God's delight in impassioned prayer:

> Even though God had already promised to send rain, and was going to do so, he nevertheless waited till Elijah prayed earnestly for it to happen. In the Bible it always seemed to be of real pleasure and value to God to do things for his people on earth, if he could first stir up people to pray for these things.[2]

Fifth: *Elijah was expectant.* Finally, Elijah's servant returned with some good news:

> It came about at the seventh time, that he said, "Behold, a cloud as small as a man's hand is coming up from the sea." (v. 44a)

There it was, a hand-sized cloud rising from the Mediterranean Sea—the portent of a magnificent storm! Despite the cloud's small-ness, Elijah expectantly told his servant,

> "Go up, say to Ahab, 'Prepare your chariot and go down, so that the heavy shower does not stop you.'"
> (v. 44b)

Not many people spying a tiny cloud in a sky as barren as the Sahara would warn of a torrential storm. But Elijah's brimming confidence wasn't pinned on a cloud; it was fastened to the promise-keeping God—the God powerful enough to send fire and gracious enough to send rain.

---

2. Ronald S. Wallace, *Readings in 1 Kings* (Grand Rapids, Mich.: William B. Eerdmans Publishing Co., 1995), p. 125.

The Promise Fulfilled

The small cloud gathered moisture, and the wind began to blow. More clouds formed, and daylight disappeared behind mammoth mountains of darkness in the sky:

> In a little while the sky grew black with clouds and wind, and there was a heavy shower. And Ahab rode and went to Jezreel. (v. 45)

Jezreel was probably Ahab's summer residence and lay about twenty miles east of Mount Carmel. Ahab had to rush there to outrun the storm before his chariot got mired in the mud. But Elijah?

> Then the hand of the Lord was on Elijah, and he girded up his loins and outran Ahab to Jezreel. (v. 46)

Elijah outran Ahab's chariot! The same divine hand that stirred the wind moved through Elijah, empowering him to run like the wind all the way to Jezreel. Elijah's overtaking Ahab's chariot communicated an unforgettable lesson to the king and all of Israel: The God who rules the elements is willing to make His power available to people of faith. The God of storm and fire is also the God of the individual.

Commentator Simon J. DeVries gives us additional insight into this scene:

> Elijah, driven by "the hand of Yahweh," runs before [Ahab], triumphantly demonstrating the right of spiritual power to dominate over the claims and pretensions of earthly institutions. But paradoxically this running shows that spiritual power does not usurp the place of earthly institutions. To run before a king is to serve him still. Thus in the end the judgment on Ahab is intended for making him a better king over the covenant people. He is being chastened and instructed, not destroyed. Whether repentance will come before a final punishment, is left untold. Ahab may not repent, but he now surely knows who is true God in Israel.[3]

3. Simon J. DeVries, *Word Biblical Commentary: 1 Kings* (Waco, Tex.: Word Books, Publisher, 1985), vol. 12, p. 219.

And this part of the story ends with a triumphant exclamation point! God has demonstrated His power and His people have returned to their covenant relationship with Him. Elijah has modeled humble prayer and embodied the personal filling of God. But one question mark remains: Will King Ahab follow suit and repent too?

The story is not over. Though Jezebel's prophets have been vanquished, the wicked queen has not. Elijah faces her next—will he have the same clear-cut victory? We'll see the surprising answer in our next chapter.

Living Insights

The New Testament remembers Elijah as "a man with a nature like ours" (James 5:17a)—weaknesses and all. His prayers flowed not from some inner talent or power but from his faith in God's promises. Our prayer and God's promises make an inseparable pair.

How can we draw our prayers more from the promises of God? Let's look at four steps.

First, *find the promise*. This is the discovery stage, where we learn which promises apply to us and what conditions they might entail. Once we locate a promise in Scripture, we should note the context carefully. Is it a universal promise, applicable to anyone? Or a personal promise, meant only for a certain individual or group at a particular time and in a unique situation? A good example of this latter type is God's promise to Joshua that He would knock down Jericho's walls if Joshua led the nation around the city seven times. We can't claim that promise for any figurative Jerichos we believe we might face.

But let's take Matthew 11:28–30 as an example of a universal promise. What do you notice about this promise? Are there any conditions?

Second, *claim the promise*. This is where we take ownership of the promise and apply it to the specifics of our situation. It is also the time to address any conditional aspects of it.

Are there any actions you may need to take to fulfill your part of the promise in Matthew 11:28–30? What characteristics of Christ must we embrace before we can enter the promise of rest?

_____

_____

_____

_____

Now that you've found the promise, fulfilled its obligations, and applied it to your situation, bring it to God in prayer.

Third, *rest in the promise.* This is the waiting stage. As a loving parent, God knows what timing is best for us. Perhaps He wants to give us some time to strengthen our trust in Him. While we wait, we must resist the temptation to get ahead of Him (see Ps. 27:14; 147:11; Lam. 3:25).

Fourth, *experience the promise.* This is the results phase. God's answer may come to us in a matter of minutes, or it may take years. As you look back over your life, what answers have you received from the Lord that came from something He promised in the Bible?

_____

_____

_____

_____

Describe your feelings when you received what God had promised.

_____

_____

_____

_____

One day we will all shout, "Worthy is the Lamb that was slain" (Rev. 5:12), acknowledging Jesus' rightful place as our Redeemer. Let's accept His invitation now to enter boldly into His presence, seeking His grace through prayer to meet our needs (Heb. 4:16).

Questions for Group Discussion

1. Try to imagine yourself as a farmer struggling to survive a drought. What would it be like to watch your crops shrivel to dust and your livestock slowly starve? What would your days be like? What fears would you have? What hope would you cling to? How would the drought impact your faith?

2. Have you ever experienced a spiritual or emotional drought—perhaps a spell of depression or hopelessness? What kept you going?

3. A dry season is a true test of faith. Can we trust God to keep His promise of rain when there isn't one cloud on the horizon? Have you struggled to keep your faith alive during dry times?

4. In his book *Elijah: A Man of Heroism and Humility*, Charles R. Swindoll comments on the reliability of God: "God keeps His promises. It's a major part of His immutable nature. He doesn't hold out hope with nice-sounding words, then renege on what He said He would do. God is neither fickle nor moody. And He never lies."[4] How did Elijah's actions demonstrate his belief in this truth about God?

5. Take some time in your group to read the following verses aloud: Psalm 103:11–13; Proverbs 3:5–6; Isaiah 41:10; Matthew 7:7–8; Romans 10:11–13; Philippians 4:19; 1 Thessalonians 4:16–17; and 1 Peter 4:12–17. Which of these promises can you cling to this week? As we close in prayer, imagine yourself as a farmer feeling that first patter of rain—God's blessing of hope.

---

4. Charles R. Swindoll, *Elijah: A Man of Heroism and Humility* (Nashville, Tenn.: Word Publishing, 2000), p. 91.

Chapter 7

SURE CURE FOR THE BLUES

1 Kings 19

In the movie version of Elijah's life (if there were such a thing), after the triumph on Mount Carmel, Elijah would run through the gates of Jezreel like a first-place marathon runner entering an Olympic stadium. Cheers would erupt from the crowds. Elijah would raise his arms in victory as he jogged past ecstatic onlookers. Background music would crescendo triumphantly from a full orchestra and chorus (remember, this is a movie). And all Israel would pour into the streets, dancing in the rain and celebrating their return to the true God.

Ahab would then arrive, pull his chariot to a stop, and quietly survey the scene. In a moving climax, the king would walk over to Elijah and embrace him; former enemies would now be fellow servants of God. And Jezebel, having heard of Baal's unmistakable defeat, would kneel before Elijah and ask him to pray to Yahweh to forgive her. Baal would be banished from the land, and God's light would shine eternally on Israel. Fade out and roll credits.

That's how we'd like the story to end, right? The hero wins the day. Enemies unite. Evil shrinks back, defeated once and for all. But the Bible is not a Hollywood script. It's a real Book about real people. And in the real world, unfortunately, many life stories don't have happy endings.

A Death Threat from Jezebel

The scenes of 1 Kings 19 trace the actions of three key people: Ahab, Jezebel, and Elijah. Let's look at the impact each had on the other.

The Weak King: Ahab

At the end of 1 Kings 18, Ahab was at a spiritual crossroads. Would he submit to the Lord and join the nation in repentance? Or would he continue in his old ways? Tragically, Ahab's fear of Jezebel overshadowed his fear of the Lord. He even seemed to have missed the point of what had happened on Mount Carmel:

Now Ahab told Jezebel all that *Elijah* had done,

56

and how he had killed all the prophets with the sword. (1 Kings 19:1, emphasis added)

Scholars Richard D. Patterson and Hermann J. Austel point out that "although Ahab had witnessed God's power in the famine and in the consuming of the sacrifice and the sending of the rain, before the imposing presence of Jezebel he could but attribute it all to Elijah, even blaming him for the death of the prophets of Baal." [1] So Ahab did not turn to Yahweh but to his dominant wife, who took sadistic charge of the situation.

The Dominant Queen: Jezebel

Enraged at Elijah for humiliating her husband and her religion, Jezebel declared her revenge on Yahweh's prophet:

> Then Jezebel sent a messenger to Elijah, saying, "So may the gods do to me and even more, if I do not make your life as the life of one of them by tomorrow about this time." (v. 2)

Why "tomorrow"? Why didn't Jezebel seize Elijah and kill him right then? Patterson and Austel reveal the queen's true aim: "What she desired was that Elijah and his God be discredited before the new converts who had aided Elijah by executing the prophets of Baal. Without a leader revolutionary movements usually stumble and fall away." [2] Sadly, Elijah went right along with her plans.

The Discouraged Prophet: Elijah

Rather than a hero's wreath, Elijah found a death threat hanging over his head. Having just experienced the power of God coursing through his veins, you'd think he would stand up to Jezebel on a mountain of unshakable faith. But Jezebel's threat toppled him:

> And [Elijah] was afraid and arose and ran for his life and came to Beersheba, which belongs to Judah, and left his servant there. (v. 3)

Elijah knew Jezebel's threat was not an empty one (see 18:4, 13),

---

1. Richard D. Patterson and Hermann J. Austel, "1, 2 Kings," in *The Expositor's Bible Commentary*, gen. ed. Frank E. Gaebelein (Grand Rapids, Mich.: Zondervan Publishing House, Regency Reference Library, 1988), vol. 4, p. 148.

2. Patterson and Austel, "1, 2 Kings," p. 148.

but he also knew the sovereign power of God. What happened? Perhaps he was stunned that the miracle on Mount Carmel didn't immediately eradicate Baalism. Maybe he thought the Lord couldn't possibly do more than He had already done to vanquish Baal— maybe evil would have the last word after all. Or he might have felt that he'd failed, that his ministry as a prophet hadn't really accomplished anything.

Whatever the case, having run to Jezreel, Elijah just kept on running. He fled first to Beersheba, which was about a hundred miles south of Jezreel, at the southernmost tip of Judah. But that still wasn't far enough. So he left his servant behind and went even farther into the wilderness, which was a "desert wasteland, the very symbol of a wasted life."[3] There he sat, all alone, under a juniper tree (19:4a).

And the man who had run for his life prayed to die:

> "It is enough; now, O Lord, take my life, for I am
> not better than my fathers." (v. 4b)

An Encounter with the Lord

With these words, the weary prophet "lay down and slept under a juniper tree" (v. 5a). He had journeyed far, and, as commentator Iain W. Provan observes, he had "been behaving somewhat like the anti-hero Jonah—travelling to a far-flung place without a divine travel permit . . . attempting to write his own contract for the job of prophet."[4] The Lord, though, is kind and understands us better than we do ourselves. Gently, He would retrieve and restore His wayward servant.

The Lord Provides

Just as He had at Cherith and Zarephath, so now the Lord supplied Elijah's needs in the desolate wilderness:

> Behold, there was an angel touching him, and he
> said to him, "Arise, eat." Then he looked and be-
> hold, there was at his head a bread cake baked on

---

3. Patterson and Austel, "1, 2 Kings," p. 149.

4. Iain W. Provan, *New International Biblical Commentary: 1 and 2 Kings* (Peabody, Mass.: Hendrickson Publishers, 1995), p. 144. Compare God's directions in 17:2–3, 8–9; and 18:1 with the lack of them in the early part of chapter 19.

hot stones, and a jar of water. So he ate and drank and lay down again. (19:5b–6)

It is beautiful to see how our God, who needs neither sleep nor nourishment, knows and cares for the physical needs of His people, isn't it? The Lord didn't rebuke or scold Elijah; He simply sent an angel with warm food and cool water. After the prophet slept again, the angel ministered to him

a second time and touched him and said, "Arise, eat, because the journey is too great for you." (v. 7)

The Lord knew where Elijah was headed—we don't know if it was part of the prophet's desperate route of escape, the Lord's chosen destination, or both. But Yahweh would watch over His servant as he made his way deep into Israel's history:

So he arose and ate and drank, and went in the strength of that food forty days and forty nights to Horeb, the mountain of God. (v. 8)

The Lord Reveals

Mount Horeb is also known by another name: Mount Sinai. It was the place where God met with Moses to make a covenant with Israel and to give them His Law (Exod. 19–24). Moses was on that mountain for forty days and nights, and there he saw the Lord (33:12–23). The Lord had told Moses, "My presence shall go with you, and I will give you rest" (v. 14)—words that perhaps echoed in Elijah's dispirited memory.

When Elijah finally arrived at Mount Horeb, "he came there to a cave and lodged there" (1 Kings 19:9a).[5] Then the Lord Himself spoke to him, again not in anger, but this time with a probing question:

"What are you doing here, Elijah?" (v. 9b)

In essence, the Lord asked him, *Why aren't you holding My banner high in Israel, Elijah? Why have you run away, Elijah? What do you want at My mountain, Elijah?*

What answer could he give? The one he did give "completely

---

5. Patterson and Austel note that "the Hebrew text says, 'He came there to *the* cave,' possibly the very 'cleft of the rock' where God had placed Moses as his glory passed by (Exod. 33:21–23)." "1, 2 Kings," p. 149.

devalued what had happened on Mt Carmel."[6] He informed God,

> "I have been very zealous for the Lord, the God of hosts; for the sons of Israel have forsaken Your covenant, torn down Your altars and killed Your prophets with the sword. And I alone am left; and they seek my life, to take it away."[7] (v. 10)

Everything was death and despair; the only positive thing Elijah could remember was "his own prophetic authority and authenticity. . . . Any prophet who sees things going badly in his ministry and as a result wants to abandon it and perhaps surrender his very life must assuredly have forgotten from whom his real strength comes."[8] It's as if Elijah told God, *I'm all You have left, Lord, and I'm not enough.* And no, he wasn't enough. But the Lord would show him who was:

> So He said, "Go forth and stand on the mountain before the Lord." And behold, the Lord was passing by! And a great and strong wind was rending the mountains and breaking in pieces the rocks before the Lord; but the Lord was not in the wind. And after the wind an earthquake, but the Lord was not in the earthquake. After the earthquake a fire, but the Lord was not in the fire. (vv. 11–12a)

Wind, earthquakes, and fire were all associated with the Lord's power and often His judgment (see Judg. 5:4–5; Ps. 11:6; 18:7–15; 68:7–8; 77:16–20; Isa. 64:1–4; Hab. 3:10a). This would have been especially true on the mountain of the covenant: "Now Mount Sinai was all in smoke because the Lord descended upon it in fire; and its smoke ascended like the smoke of a furnace, and the whole mountain quaked violently" (Exod. 19:18). But this time, the Lord didn't choose to reveal Himself in those elements. Instead, He chose

---

6. John J. Bimson, "1 and 2 Kings," in the *New Bible Commentary: 21st Century Edition*, 4th ed., rev., edited by D. A. Carson, R. T. France, J. A. Motyer, and G. J. Wenham (Downers Grove, Ill.: InterVarsity Press, 1994), p. 360.

7. J. Robert Vannoy observes that "whereas Moses had interceded for Israel when they sinned with the golden calf (Ex 32:11–13), Elijah condemned the Israelites for breaking the covenant." Note on 1 Kings 19:10, in *The NIV Study Bible*, gen. ed. Kenneth L. Barker (Grand Rapids, Mich.: Zondervan Bible Publishers, 1985), p. 514.

8. Simon J. DeVries, *Word Biblical Commentary: 1 Kings* (Waco, Tex.: Word Books, Publisher, 1985), vol. 12, pp. 236–37.

something Elijah did not expect but recognized just the same:

> And after the fire a sound of gentle blowing. When
> Elijah heard it, he wrapped his face in his mantle
> and went out and stood in the entrance of the cave.
> (1 Kings 19:12b–13a)

Commentator Gene Rice describes this "gentle blowing" as "a filled, gripping, perceptible silence or stillness."[9] John J. Bimson calls it "a brief sound of silence."[10] And Paul R. House notes that "God speaks in a quiet voice here to a prophet drained of strength."[11] Whatever the exact sound might have been, it was more of a whisper of grace than a storm of judgment. Lightning bolts of judgment might have been what Elijah was hoping for—the Lord should have just zapped Ahab and Jezebel, he may have wished.

But the Lord frequently chooses to work quietly rather than with spectacular miracles. This is something the disheartened prophet was apparently reluctant to grasp. Out of the full silence, the Lord again asked him,

> "What are you doing here, Elijah?" (v. 13b)

And Elijah gave the same answer as before:

> "I have been very zealous for the Lord, the God of
> hosts; for the sons of Israel have forsaken Your cov-
> enant, torn down Your altars and killed Your proph-
> ets with the sword. And I alone am left; and they
> seek my life, to take it away." (v. 14)

What would it take to get Elijah out of this fearful, despairing rut? A restored perspective and sense of purpose, which is what the Lord provided for him next.

The Lord Commissions

As if to reassure Elijah that He was sovereign not only over Israel but all the nations, the Lord commissioned him "to anoint a

9. Gene Rice, *Nations under God: A Commentary on the Book of 1 Kings*, International Theological Commentary Series (Grand Rapids, Mich.: William B. Eerdmans Publishing Co., 1990), p. 160.

10. Bimson, "1 and 2 Kings," p. 360.

11. Paul R. House, *1, 2 Kings*, The New American Commentary Series (Nashville, Tenn.: Broadman and Holman Publishers, 1995), vol. 8, p. 224.

new generation of political and religious leaders."[12]

> The Lord said to him, "Go, return on your way to the wilderness of Damascus, and when you have arrived, you shall anoint Hazael king over Aram; and Jehu the son of Nimshi you shall anoint king over Israel; and Elisha the son of Shaphat of Abel-meholah you shall anoint as prophet in your place. It shall come about, the one who escapes from the sword of Hazael, Jehu shall put to death, and the one who escapes from the sword of Jehu, Elisha shall put to death." (vv. 15–17)

With these words, Elijah learned that God's plans were bigger than him and would continue far beyond his ministry. God would not fail—His victory over Baal would be complete in time. But Elijah needed to see that, although God had a place and a purpose for him in His plans, Elijah played only *one* part—the Lord of Hosts did not depend on him entirely. Elijah seemed to have forgotten what Obadiah had told him: "I hid a hundred prophets of the Lord by fifties in a cave, and provided them with bread and water" (18:13b). His contention that he "alone [was] left" (19:10, 14) was simply not true, and the Lord gently corrected him:

> "Yet I will leave 7,000 in Israel, all the knees that have not bowed to Baal and every mouth that has not kissed him." (v. 18)

The situation in Israel was not out of control; the Lord had preserved a remnant faithful to Him. Elijah was part of that remnant, and much of his focus would now turn to preparing the way for those who would do the Lord's work after him.[13]

With this commission from the Lord, it was time for Elijah to get back to work. He had a ministry to fulfill, and his first task was to ordain his successor:

> So he departed from there and found Elisha the

---

12. Vannoy, note on map of "Lives of Elijah and Elisha" in *The NIV Study Bible*, p. 513.

13. As Moses prepared the way for Joshua, and John the Baptist prepared the way for Jesus, so Elijah prepared the way for Elisha. It is significant that Joshua's, Elisha's, and Jesus' names have a similar meaning: Joshua—"The Lord is salvation" or "The Lord saves"; Elisha—"God is salvation" or "God saves"; and Jesus—"The Lord saves." Jesus' ministry is foreshadowed in interesting ways by Elisha's life.

son of Shaphat, while he was plowing with twelve
pairs of oxen[14] before him, and he with the twelfth.
And Elijah passed over to him and threw his mantle
on him. (v. 19)

This was the first time Elijah's mantle of authority would rest
on Elisha's shoulders—the next time would be right after Elijah
was taken up to heaven, thus transferring his position to Elisha
permanently (see 2 Kings 2:11–15). For now, the two would shoul-
der the ministry of Yahweh together, which was something Elisha
was eager to do. After cutting his ties to his family by kissing them
good-bye (1 Kings 19:20), Elisha literally burned the connections
to his past in a public declaration of his new vocation:

So [Elisha] . . . took the pair of oxen and sacrificed
them and boiled their flesh with the implements of
the oxen, and gave it to the people and they ate.
Then he arose and followed Elijah and ministered
to him. (v. 21)

With Elisha's encouraging presence by his side, Elijah was now
ready to return to Israel and await another day when he would once
again face Ahab—this time without fire from heaven but with a
somber word from the Lord.

Living Insights

Though most of us won't become depressed from a wicked
queen's threat to kill us, we *will* face times of discouragement in
our work for the Lord. So it may be helpful for us to look at some
of the factors that probably contributed to Elijah's depression. By
becoming aware of them and the ways God dealt with Elijah, we
can learn how to regain our footing and continue to find meaning
in our service to the Lord.

1. *Elijah was not thinking realistically or clearly, so the Lord gently
corrected his perspective.* Was Jezebel stronger than Yahweh? Of
course not! Was Elijah the only believer left? Not at all—besides
the hidden hundred (18:13), the Lord revealed that there were

---

14. Twelve pairs of oxen showed that Elisha and his family were rich.

seven thousand more who had remained faithful to Him. Fear distorted Elijah's thinking, and he ran instead of praying.

Have you ever followed in Elijah's stressed-out steps? What happened, and how did God get you back on track?

_____

_____

_____

2. *Elijah had separated himself from relationships that strengthen, so the Lord gave him Elisha as a companion.* Elijah left his servant at Beersheba and journeyed into the wilderness alone. The servant was faithful—he didn't abandon Elijah, but Elijah abandoned him. To prevent the "I alone am left" feelings from returning, God directed Elijah to take on Elisha as an apprentice and partner.

When fear, confusion, and despair invade your life, do you withdraw as Elijah did? Does your depression wind up feeding on your loneliness? How has God helped you out of this painful place in the past?

_____

_____

_____

3. *Elijah was caught in the aftermath of a great victory, so the Lord showed him that His kingdom also advances in quiet, sometimes unnoticed ways.* Everything in Elijah's life had been geared to prepare him for the confrontation on Mount Carmel. Surely Baalism would be destroyed for all time after that! But it wasn't. Elijah might have wondered, "Has my whole life been a waste?" The Lord reassured him it was not by inviting him to see that He is present even in a silence that can easily escape notice. Ordaining others was not spectacular work, but in the ordinariness of the political realm and with the unseen forces of heaven, they would complete the work Elijah had begun.

Have you ever hit bottom after soaring high for the Lord? Do you seek God's spectacular acts more than His subtle ones? How have you encountered God in quiet, ordinary ways?

_____

4. *Elijah was physically exhausted and emotionally spent, so the Lord let him rest and gave him food for his journey.* The stress and adrenaline from Mount Carmel, Jezebel's unopposed opposition, and his long trek into the wilderness drained Elijah. In his depleted state, all he could do was sleep. And the Lord let him. Unlike His dealings with His other runaway prophet, Jonah (who made his decision to obey God in the odoriferous belly of a huge fish), the Lord took gentle, patient care of Elijah. The prophet slept twice, ate two angel-provided meals, and met God in quiet stillness.

When you run into depression, do you pay attention to getting the sleep and nourishment you need? Do you think God sees you as being disobedient, ready to cast you overboard like Jonah? Or do you know He realizes that discouragement and disobedience are different, and that He will treat you gently, as He treated Elijah?

5. *Elijah had submitted to self-pity, so the Lord had him submit to Himself again.* "O Lord, take my life, for I am not better than my fathers" (v. 4). But who said he had to be better than his fathers? "I alone am left" (vv. 10, 14). But he wasn't. Elijah had "underrated his own achievement and undervalued the contribution of others."[15] So the Lord probed his motives twice: "What are you doing here, Elijah?" (vv. 9, 13), He showed His awesome power (vv. 11–12), and He gave him a command to fulfill (vv. 15–17).

When you find yourself mucking about in self-pity, have you landed there because you've failed to meet some unrealistically high standards you've set for yourself? Have you discounted other people's contributions? How does the Lord usually get you back on solid ground?

15. Bimson, "1 and 2 Kings," p. 360.

A big part of Elijah's problem was that he lost sight of the Lord. So the next time circumstances threaten to knock you down and hold you there, remember to *turn to the Lord first*. He won't tear you apart with wind, earthquakes, and fire; He'll draw you to Himself in quietness, gentleness, and care. And He'll have a plan that's bigger than your circumstances could ever be.

 ## *Questions for Group Discussion*

1. In 1 Kings 18, Elijah stood tall before hundreds of his enemies; in chapter 19, his knees buckled before Jezebel. In chapter 18, Elijah ran in victory; in chapter 19, he retreated in defeat. In chapter 18, Elijah prayed for the life of his people; in chapter 19, he prayed for his own death. Two chapters—one marked by faith, the other by fear. As you thumb through the pages of your life's story, can you find two similarly incongruous chapters?

2. We've looked at some of the factors that might have contributed to the dramatic shift in Elijah's life. What factors have you seen in yours?

3. Elijah's sudden fear and subsequent depression surprise us. Is there anything about God's response to Elijah that surprises you?

4. What message did God communicate to Elijah about Himself through the wind, earthquake, fire, and finally the gentle sound (19:11–13)?

5. What message does He want to communicate to you when you feel discouraged and afraid?

Chapter 8

WHEN GOD SAYS, "THAT'S ENOUGH!"

1 Kings 21

As if to underscore His message that Elijah wasn't the only faithful prophet at His disposal (1 Kings 19:16, 18), the Lord used two unnamed prophets to deliver His divine messages to Ahab in 1 Kings 20.

The first prophet had three messages for Ahab. In the first, he told the besieged king that the Lord would give him victory over Ben-hadad, king of neighboring Aram, and his superior forces. Why? So Ahab would know that Yahweh was the Lord (v. 13).

Then the prophet returned with a second message: Ben-hadad would try to lay waste to Israel again, so Ahab needed to prepare his forces. Ahab again followed the Lord's instructions, and sure enough, Ben-hadad came back for more. He thought Israel's God was only a god of the hills, so he decided to attack Israel on the plains.

This prompted the prophet's third message, which assured Ahab of victory once more. The Lord wanted to show Ben-hadad that He was Lord of all, not just one area, like a local Baal, and He wanted to reaffirm to Ahab that He was indeed the one true God (v. 28). This would be a kind of holy war, where Yahweh would protect His people and, in doing so, make Himself known as the Lord (a theme that's hard to miss).

Ahab followed the divine strategy again—up to a point. Israel drove out the Aramean forces, but instead of relying solely on the Lord's protection, Ahab sought to make himself secure by establishing a treaty with the very king who sought to destroy him. Like King Saul, who spared the life of Agag against the Lord's command (1 Sam. 15), Ahab departed from the Lord's counsel and followed his own course.

Enter the Lord's second prophet, this time with a word of doom:

> "Thus says the Lord, 'Because you have let go out of your hand the man whom I had devoted to destruction, therefore your life shall go for his life, and your people for his people.'" (1 Kings 20:42)

Did Ahab grieve and repent? Not on your life! He went home "sullen and vexed" (v. 43)—a sour, stubborn attitude that will wreak havoc in chapter 21. Here the Lord's most fearsome prophet, Elijah, will reenter the scene and pronounce a second, frighteningly detailed judgment on this sinful king and his evil wife. The Lord God— who is "compassionate and gracious, slow to anger, and abounding in lovingkindness" (Exod. 34:6)—will finally have had enough.[1]

The Corruption of Justice

The sin of covetousness started an avalanche of other sins in this story. Covetousness respects self—and self only. Others get savagely plowed under in its path, as did an unobtrusive, God-fearing farmer named Naboth when Ahab wanted his vineyard.

The Conflict

Ahab had his eye on a nice tract of land next to his summer palace in Jezreel. It was owned, however, by someone else—Naboth, a simple, devout follower of Yahweh. Ahab approached him as a potential buyer, giving what he must have thought was a generous offer:

> "Give me your vineyard, that I may have it for a vegetable garden because it is close beside my house, and I will give you a better vineyard than it in its place; if you like, I will give you the price of it in money." (1 Kings 21:2)

On the surface, Ahab's offer seemed reasonable. Which is why Naboth's answer surprised him: "The Lord forbid me that I should give you the inheritance of my fathers" (v. 3). Why did Naboth feel so strongly? Commentator Gene Rice explains:

> Naboth claimed the right to keep his vineyard because it was the inheritance (*nahalah*) of his ancestors. Land was not a private possession and commercial commodity in Israel but a gift and trust held

---

1. As is shown throughout Kings and Chronicles, God's desired approach with sinners is to get their attention, lead them to repentance, and graciously forgive them (see also Paul's testimony in 1 Tim. 1:12–16). However, the Lord will not allow sin to go on forever. There is a limit even to His patience (see Gen. 19:1–29; Num. 14; 1 Sam. 15; Prov. 6:12–15; 29:1; Acts 5:1–11).

from God, the real owner (Lev. 25:23), for the sake of the family (Num. 27:1–11; 36:1–12). The vineyard was an indulgence to Ahab, but to Naboth it was his link with his ancestors, the source of his identity, livelihood, and position in the community. Here were his roots, and because of his ownership of this land he enjoyed the rights and privileges of a free citizen.[2]

The Anger

The story should have ended here, but tragically, it didn't. Instead of apologizing to Naboth and the Lord,

> Ahab came into his house sullen and vexed because of the word which Naboth the Jezreelite had spoken to him. . . . And he lay down on his bed and turned away his face and ate no food. (1 Kings 21:4)

"Sullen and vexed" again. How childish! He sulked and pouted and threw a tantrum. His behavior soon captured his wife's attention—which it was probably designed to do—and when she heard his pitiful story (minus Naboth's reason), she decided to take matters into her own hands:

> Jezebel his wife said to him, "Do you now reign over Israel? Arise, eat bread, and let your heart be joyful; I will give you the vineyard of Naboth the Jezreelite." (v. 7)

In Jezebel's mind, a king had a sovereign right to do whatever he pleased, regardless. But "an Israelite king was bound by the law of Yahweh as much as any of his subjects (Dt. 17:18–20)."[3] That's why Ahab didn't simply seize Naboth's land. And neither would Jezebel. She was too crafty for that.

2. Gene Rice, *Nations under God: A Commentary on the Book of 1 Kings*, International Theological Commentary Series (Grand Rapids, Mich.: William B. Eerdmans Publishing Co., 1990), p. 176.

3. John J. Bimson, "1 and 2 Kings," in the *New Bible Commentary: 21st Century Edition*, 4th ed., rev., edited by D. A. Carson, R. T. France, J. A. Motyer, and G. J. Wenham (Downers Grove, Ill.: InterVarsity Press, 1994), p. 361.

The Conspiracy to Commit Murder

Knowing something about Israel's legal practices and a little about mob psychology, Jezebel wrote letters (in Ahab's name and with his seal) to the elders and nobles in Jezreel, directing them to

> "proclaim a fast and seat Naboth at the head of the people; and seat two worthless men before him, and let them testify against him, saying, 'You cursed God and the king.' Then take him out and stone him to death." (vv. 9–10)

Why would Jezebel choose a fast? A fast was usually "called as a result of some misfortune . . . interpreted to be due to God's displeasure," Gene Rice tells us.

> The purpose of the fast was to summon the community to repentance, to learn wherein God was displeased. . . . A fast thus created a setting and atmosphere that made it easy to carry out Jezebel's plot by identifying Naboth as the culprit responsible for the calamity. . . . By setting Naboth in a prominent position . . . it was easy to make him a target.[4]

As a sad testimony to Ahab and Jezebel's legacy of moral decline, the nobles cooperated, the false witnesses lied, and Naboth and his sons were murdered (vv. 11–13; 2 Kings 9:26).[5]

The Theft

When Jezebel received word that Naboth and his family had been stoned to death, she told her husband:

> "Arise, take possession of the vineyard of Naboth, the Jezreelite, which he refused to give you for money; for Naboth is not alive, but dead." (1 Kings 21:15b)

---

4. Rice, *Nations under God*, p. 177.

5. Of this episode commentator J. Robinson notes: "All those who had played any part in the legal farce in deference to or fear of the king had been corrupted. God's purpose for the law was to ensure that society was righteous, but used thus as an instrument of royal power, it destroyed the moral basis of society." *The First Book of Kings*, The Cambridge Bible Commentary Series (London, England: Cambridge University Press, 1972), p. 237.

With Naboth and all the heirs who had any claim to the property out of the way, Ahab could now have his vegetable patch. He had to have known that Jezebel was responsible for Naboth's death, and his tacit consent to let her handle the matter made him just as guilty of the murder as she. Without asking questions, then, he went to take possession of the land (v. 16). But Ahab and Jezebel overlooked one obstacle to their plans: Yahweh, who watches over the poor and needy and upholds justice (Deut. 16:19–20; Ps. 37:28; Prov. 17:5; 22:22–23; Isa. 10:1–4; Jer. 9:24).

The Retribution of the Lord

The Lord had been tracking this fiasco, and He had had enough. He summoned Elijah and gave him this message to deliver to Ahab:

> "'Thus says the Lord, "Have you murdered and also taken possession?"' And you shall speak to him, saying, 'Thus says the Lord, "In the place where the dogs licked up the blood of Naboth the dogs will lick up your blood, even yours."'"[6] (1 Kings 21:19)

The Confrontation

Ahab was not overjoyed to see Elijah picking his way toward him through Naboth's vineyard: "Have you found me, O my enemy?" (v. 20a).

"I have found you," Elijah answered, "because you have sold yourself to do evil in the sight of the Lord" (v. 20b). Instead of serving the Lord, Ahab had become the slave of evil—he had sold out to wickedness to get what he wanted.[7] And Elijah wasted no time delivering the Lord's decree:

> "Behold, I will bring evil upon you, and will utterly sweep you away, and will cut off from Ahab every male, both bond and free in Israel; and I will make

6. Commentator J. Robinson tells us that dogs, in that ancient time and place, lived off "the refuse of society." So this was a sign that Ahab would die "as one cast out by both God and men." *The First Book of Kings*, p. 239.

7. See Rice, *Nations under God*, p. 179; R. Laird Harris, Gleason L. Archer Jr., and Bruce K. Waltke, eds., *Theological Wordbook of the Old Testament* (Chicago, Ill.: Moody Press, 1980), vol. 1, pp. 504–5; C. F. Keil, *I and II Kings, I and II Chronicles, Ezra, Nehemiah, Esther*, vol. 3 in *Commentary on the Old Testament in Ten Volumes* (reprint, Grand Rapids, Mich.: William B. Eerdmans Publishing Co., 1982), p. 272.

your house like the house of Jeroboam the son of Nebat, and like the house of Baasha the son of Ahijah, because of the provocation with which you have provoked Me to anger, and because you have made Israel sin. Of Jezebel also has the Lord spoken, saying, 'The dogs will eat Jezebel in the district of Jezreel.' The one belonging to Ahab, who dies in the city, the dogs will eat, and the one who dies in the field the birds of heaven will eat." (vv. 21–24)

Ahab's wife and descendants would not even have a decent burial, let alone a royal one. Commentator J. Robinson observes:

> The threat to Ahab's family is of total annihilation. The name and memory of Ahab was to be removed root and branch from Israel, and all his family were to die in such a way that it would be clear to the nation that the whole family had been rejected by God. Their bodies would be treated as refuse.[8]

This was a fearful judgment, but Ahab himself had chosen the path that would lead to those consequences. As the writer of 1 Kings observed:

> Surely there was no one like Ahab who sold himself to do evil in the sight of the Lord, because Jezebel his wife incited him. He acted very abominably in following idols, according to all that the Amorites [Canaanites] had done, whom the Lord cast out before the sons of Israel. (vv. 25–26)

The Temporary Reprieve

Unlike his sullen response to the judgment pronounced on him by the unnamed prophet (20:42–43), this time Ahab repented. He tore his clothes, put on sackcloth, fasted, and "went about despondently" (21:27). He finally humbled himself before the Lord, but now it was too late. The Lord's judgment was irrevocable. However, the Lord always responds to humble repentance, and He extended a grace to Ahab:

> Then the word of the Lord came to Elijah the Tishbite, saying, "Do you see how Ahab has humbled

8. Robinson, *The First Book of Kings*, p. 240.

himself before Me? Because he has humbled himself before Me, I will not bring the evil in his days, but I will bring the evil upon his house in his son's days." (vv. 28–29)

The Fulfillment of the Judgment

The Lord, of course, was true to His word.

In 1 Kings 22, Ahab decided to go to war against Aram, spurred on by a bevy of lying prophets. He tried to get around the message of Micaiah, the one true prophet of the Lord present, by disguising himself and having his ally, King Jehoshaphat of Judah, be the only target in royal attire. But Ahab couldn't hide from God. A soldier "drew his bow at random" and hit Ahab in the one vital place his armor didn't cover. He bled to death in his chariot, and when it was taken to be washed, "the dogs licked up his blood" at a pool where shrine prostitutes bathed (vv. 34, 38).

His son Ahaziah would die next, as we'll see in our following chapter on 2 Kings 1. His brother Jehoram (also known as Joram) would succeed him and be the next to die. Jehu, of whom the Lord prophesied in 1 Kings 19:17, shot an arrow through Jehoram's back that went deep into his heart, and his body was thrown into "the field of Naboth the Jezreelite" (2 Kings 9:22–26). Jehu then killed Ahab's grandson, King Ahaziah of Judah (v. 27; Ahab's daughter Athaliah married King Jehoshaphat's son).

Then it was Jezebel's turn. Several court officials threw the queen out of the window from which she'd been looking down at Jehu. Her death was as brutal as her life had been: "Some of her blood was sprinkled on the wall and on the horses, and [Jehu] trampled her under foot" (v. 33). A little while later, when they went to bury her, all they found was her skull, feet, and the palms of her hands (v. 35). The dogs had torn apart and devoured her body, just as the Lord had decreed (vv. 36–37).

Finally, Jehu slaughtered every relative of Ahab, as well as his chief men, his friends and acquaintances, and his priests (10:11). Ahab's murderous daughter Athaliah was the last to be put to death (11:13–16). Ahab's house was utterly destroyed.

The Lessons for Today

One overarching theme of the incident at Naboth's vineyard is summed up by commentator Iain W. Provan:

Worship and ethics are but two sides of the same coin. . . . Abandonment of God . . . inevitably leads to abandonment of righteousness; we see the reality of this in 1 Kings 21—in this society given over to idol-worship, covetousness . . . leads on to false testimony, murder, and theft.[9]

And ultimately, to judgment.

What can we learn about how God deals with us from how He dealt with Ahab? Three things:

- *There is an end to God's patience, and no one knows when it will come.* As the writer of Hebrews said, "Today if you hear His voice, Do not harden your hearts" (Heb. 4:7).

- *God keeps His promise, and no one stops it.* The Lord is patient with us, "not wishing for any to perish but for all to come to repentance" (2 Pet. 3:9). But He will not let us get away with sin: "Do not be deceived, God is not mocked; for whatever a man sows, this he will also reap" (Gal. 6:7).

- *God acknowledges humility, and no one should refuse it.* As James advises us, "God is opposed to the proud, but gives grace to the humble. Submit therefore to God" (James 4:6b–7a). The Lord longs to revive a broken and contrite heart (see Isa. 57:15).

If we'll take these lessons to heart, we will never have to hear God say to us, "That's enough!"

Living Insights

Gene Rice observes, "When the First Commandment is not honored the other commandments suffer."[10] How true! When we put other gods before the Lord—in our society, these might include success, wealth, status, possessions, independence, education, or science, just to name a few—we're often tempted to do whatever it takes to serve them. Ahab did, with disastrous results.

---

9. Iain W. Provan, *1 and 2 Kings*, New International Biblical Commentary Series (Peabody, Mass.: Hendrickson Publishers, 1995), p. 158.

10. Rice, *Nations under God*, p. 180.

Are there any aspects of Ahab's life that you see creeping into yours? Do you ever try to serve the Lord *and* something (or someone) else? What might that be?

_____

_____

_____

What choices have you made to serve this "god"? Are these choices consistent with what the Lord expects of you?

_____

_____

_____

Has God been trying to get your attention and lead you back to Himself? How has He tried to do this?

_____

_____

_____

What's been your response to His efforts? Have you been sullen and vexed, like Ahab, or have you recognized His grace and come back to Him?

_____

_____

_____

The Lord tried over and over again to get Ahab's attention, but Ahab continually hardened his heart. Sadly, he only repented when it was too late. Let's learn from Ahab's mistakes. If you're straying from the Lord, even in what seems like the smallest way, turn back to Him, won't you? As a later prophet revealed of Him:

> "For I have no pleasure in the death of anyone who dies," declares the Lord God. "Therefore, repent and live." (Ezek. 18:32; see also Mic. 7:18)

Questions for Group Discussion

1. What do you think is the link between what we serve and how we live?

2. Scholar Raymond B. Dillard notes that "it is human nature always to want more." Then he asks a good question: "What means are you tempted to employ to get what you want in life?"[11]

3. Why did the crime against Naboth and his family call down such a harsh judgment from God? How does it connect with God's responsibilities for government leaders (see Deut. 17:14–20; Ps. 72)?

4. Do you think the Lord was fair to punish Ahab for the conspiracy Jezebel engineered? Why or why not?

5. Do you think it was fair of the Lord to wipe out every member of Ahab's house? Why or why not?

6. What have you learned from this story about the Lord and His values?

11. Raymond B. Dillard, *Faith in the Face of Apostasy: The Gospel according to Elijah and Elisha*, The Gospel according to the Old Testament Series (Phillipsburg, N.J.: Presbyterian and Reformed Publishing, 1999), p. 72.

Chapter 9

WATCH OUT
FOR THE ENEMY
2 Kings 1

Some people never learn, do they? The newspapers run story after story about people who get killed trying to beat the train across the tracks, yet many still try it. Each year in the United States alone, more than 400,000 smokers die an awful death from their habit, but people continue to light up. Hundreds of thousands of children watch their parents die from years of drug or alcohol abuse, but many of them turn around and become addicts themselves.

Ahab's son Ahaziah was a person who never learned. He surely knew of his father's encounters with Elijah—how the kingdom had suffered under a drought for three long years. How Elijah's God had thoroughly shown up Baal. How Baal's prophets had been slaughtered at Elijah's command. How Elijah's final prophecy about Ahab's death had come to pass, right down to the dogs licking up his blood (1 Kings 22:38).

This was a man who had seen the one true God work directly with his family. But did Ahaziah learn from this? Nope.

When Ahaziah succeeded his father, he became just one more in Israel's line of evil kings. A change of rulers may have taken place, but Ahaziah didn't stray from the dark religious system of his parents:

> Ahaziah the son of Ahab became king over Israel in Samaria in the seventeenth year of Jehoshaphat king of Judah, and he reigned two years over Israel. He did evil in the sight of the Lord and walked in the way of his father and in the way of his mother and in the way of Jeroboam the son of Nebat, who caused Israel to sin. So he served Baal and worshiped him and provoked the Lord God of Israel to anger, according to all that his father had done. (vv. 51–53)

After Ahab's example, his son should have known that "it is a terrifying thing to fall into the hands of the living God" (Heb. 10:31). But some people never learn, do they?

Ahaziah's Disastrous Decision

The Lord punished Ahaziah for his wickedness in a number of ways.[1] Ahaziah's attempt to form a commercial alliance with King Jehoshaphat of Judah was disastrously thwarted (see 1 Kings 22:47–49; 2 Chron. 20:35–37). He lost control of the vassal state Moab when its people rebelled (2 Kings 1:1). And then he had a debilitating—and ultimately fatal—injury:

> Ahaziah fell through the lattice in his upper chamber which was in Samaria, and became ill. (v. 2a)

Bedridden from his fall, Ahaziah worried that he might not ever recover. So he decided to take matters into his own hands and see exactly what the future held:

> So he sent messengers and said to them, "Go, inquire of Baal-zebub, the god of Ekron, whether I will recover from this sickness." (v. 2b)

Little did he realize that, by seeking out the deadly enemies of God, he had just signed his own death warrant.

Baal-zebub's Demonic Identity

Just who was this "Baal-zebub" that Ahaziah sought? The literal translation of his name means "Baal of flies" or "Lord of flies." Old-time scholars such as C. F. Keil believed that this god was "represented as a fly, as a fly-idol," who could both send diseases and take them away.[2]

More modern scholarship, however, takes a different view. Most commentators today propose that Baal-zebub is a corrupted form of Baal-zebul, which meant "Prince Baal" or "glorious Baal." Raymond B. Dillard explains that "by exchanging one letter for another (the final *l* for a *b*), the scribes may have deliberately and pejoratively distorted the god's true name both as a source of humor and as a

---

1. See Richard D. Patterson and Hermann J. Austel, "1, 2 Kings," in *The Expositor's Bible Commentary*, gen. ed. Frank E. Gaebelein (Grand Rapids, Mich.: Zondervan Publishing House, Regency Reference Library, 1988), vol. 4, 170.

2. C. F. Keil, *I and II Kings, I and II Chronicles, Ezra, Nehemiah, Esther*, vol. 3 in *Commentary on the Old Testament in Ten Volumes* (reprint, Grand Rapids, Mich.: William B. Eerdmans Publishing Co., 1982), p. 285. Keil and his partner Franz Delitzsch wrote their renowned commentaries on the Old Testament between 1861 and 1875.

way of stating their own estimate of this deity's worth."[3]

In light of Yahweh's power, the writer of 2 Kings viewed this idol as insubstantial; but no biblical writer took lightly the demonic force behind the idols (see 1 Cor. 10:19–20). Iain W. Provan notes that "the OT figure of Baal stands explicitly behind the NT figure of Satan."[4] In Jesus' day, the name Beelzebul was the Greek equivalent of Baal-zebub, and he was recognized as "the ruler of the demons" (see Matt. 12:24; Mark 3:22; Luke 11:15).

In effect, Ahaziah wanted the Prince of Darkness to tell him his future. With Satan, however, there is no future.

Elijah's Fiery Rebuke

What would Ahaziah's messengers learn from the demon of Ekron? Nothing—because they'd never reach that Philistine city. The Lord would block their path with an immovable object: His prophet Elijah.

God's Message

To remind Ahaziah which God truly ruled over life and death, the Lord entrusted Elijah with this message:

> The angel of the Lord said to Elijah the Tishbite, "Arise, go up to meet the messengers of the king of Samaria and say to them, 'Is it because there is no God in Israel that you are going to inquire of Baal-zebub, the god of Ekron?' Now therefore thus says the Lord, 'You shall not come down from the bed where you have gone up, but you shall surely die.'"
> Then Elijah departed. (2 Kings 1:3–4)

3. Raymond B. Dillard, *Faith in the Face of Apostasy: The Gospel according to Elijah and Elisha*, The Gospel according to the Old Testament Series (Phillipsburg, N.J.: Presbyterian and Reformed Publishing, 1999), pp. 76–77. See also T. R. Hobbs, *Word Biblical Commentary: 2 Kings* (Waco, Tex.: Word Books, Publisher, 1985), vol. 13, p. 8; J. Robinson, *The Second Book of Kings*, The Cambridge Bible Commentary Series (London, England: Cambridge University Press, 1976), p. 18; Paul R. House, *1, 2 Kings*, The New American Commentary Series (Nashville, Tenn.: Broadman and Holman Publishers, 1995), vol. 8, p. 243; Iain W. Provan, *1 and 2 Kings*, New International Biblical Commentary Series (Peabody, Mass.: Hendrickson Publishers, 1995), p. 170; John J. Bimson, "1 and 2 Kings," in *New Biblical Commentary: 21st Century Edition*, 4th ed., rev., gen. ed. D. A. Carson, R. T. France, J. A. Motyer, and G. J. Wenham (Downers Grove, Ill.: InterVarsity Press, 1994), p. 363; and J. Robert Vannoy, note on Judges 10:6, in *The NIV Study Bible*, gen. ed. Kenneth L. Barker (Grand Rapids, Mich.: Zondervan Bible Publishers, 1985), p. 347.

4. Provan, *1 and 2 Kings*, p. 170.

Ahaziah's Messengers

When God's messenger confronted Ahaziah's messengers, the king's men immediately returned to the palace. Sensing that something must be wrong for them to have come back so prematurely, the king asked, "Why have you returned?" (v. 5). They answered, "A man came up to meet us . . ." and repeated Elijah's message word for word (v. 6).

Ahaziah, with a sneaking suspicion, prodded them for more information:

> "What kind of man was he who came up to meet you and spoke these words to you?" (v. 7)

And they filled in the blanks:

> "He was a hairy man with a leather girdle bound about his loins." And [Ahaziah] said, "It is Elijah the Tishbite." (v. 8)

A growl of recognition marked the king's voice. His family had problems with this man before; he was always standing in the way of what they wanted. And now this. Ahaziah decided to nullify Elijah's message by overpowering the prophet. But he would soon learn that God's word "cannot be brought under human control."[5]

> Then the king sent to him a captain of fifty with his fifty. And he went up to him, and behold, he was sitting on the top of the hill. And he said to him, "O man of God, the king says, 'Come down.'" Elijah replied to the captain of fifty, "If I am a man of God, let fire come down from heaven and consume you and your fifty." Then fire came down from heaven and consumed him and his fifty. (vv. 9–10)

The king's messenger ordered the man of God to come down, but the Lord's messenger commanded the fire of God to come down. Why did the Lord use such a severe penalty? Raymond B. Dillard explains:

> The messenger had the authority of the one who sent him. . . . The problem here was that the prophet

---

5. Provan, *1 and 2 Kings*, p. 169.

was the messenger of God. Just as Ahaziah's messengers enjoyed the power and respect due to their king, so too Elijah commanded the respect and reverence due to the One who sent him. The king was about to learn that no one could command God.[6]

Unfortunately for his soldiers, Ahaziah was slow to learn. He sent a second company, and this captain conveyed an even more forceful message: "Come down quickly" (v. 11). But fire again came down instead of Elijah (v. 12). Amazingly, the hard-headed king sent a third squad of fifty—he still thought that a king outranked a prophet on his strategic chessboard, as if the Power behind Elijah didn't exist.

The third captain, however, showed more sense:

> He came and bowed down on his knees before Elijah, and begged him and said to him, "O man of God, please let my life and the lives of these fifty servants of yours be precious in your sight. Behold fire came down from heaven and consumed the first two captains of fifty with their fifties; but now let my life be precious in your sight." (vv. 13–14)

Finally, here was someone who reverenced the Lord by respecting His prophet. So Elijah went with him—but only at God's command, not Ahaziah's:

> The angel of the Lord said to Elijah, "Go down with him; do not be afraid of him." So he arose and went down with him to the king. (v. 15)

The humble captain relaxed, and everyone, including Elijah, walked to Samaria to see the king.

What must Ahaziah have thought as this fiery prophet approached him? This would be their first meeting, and it would also be their last.

Elijah's Message

In his statement to the stubborn king, Elijah reiterated a penetrating rhetorical question: *Is there no God in Israel?* (see also vv. 3, 6). The only answer was, "Of course!" But Ahaziah refused to learn

---

6. Dillard, *Faith in the Face of Apostasy*, p. 78.

this, so judgment was his lot:

> Then [Elijah] said to him, "Thus says the Lord, 'Be-
> cause you have sent messengers to inquire of Baal-
> zebub, the god of Ekron—is it because there is no
> God in Israel to inquire of His word?—therefore you
> shall not come down from the bed where you have
> gone up, but shall surely die.'" (v. 16)

Fatal words. "Ahaziah, you have substituted the true for the
false. You have turned to the world's solutions and rejected the
Lord." And the consequences swiftly followed:

> So Ahaziah died according to the word of the
> Lord which Elijah had spoken. And because he had
> no son, Jehoram became king in his place in the
> second year of Jehoram the son of Jehoshaphat, king
> of Judah. (vv. 17–18)

Timely Lessons for Today

Many people seek to know the future through present-day Baal-
zebubs, such as mediums, astrology, palmistry, tarot cards, and Sa-
tanism. But these paths of darkness lead only to a dead end. From
the Lord's confrontation of Ahaziah we can learn—if we're
willing—at least three lessons that can strengthen our resolve to
never dabble in the occult.

First: *God is displeased with any occult involvement.* Scripture gives
ample warning: The occult, whether in the form of white or black
magic, Ouija boards, spiritism, seances, or any other expressions of
darkness, is off-limits to a person following the Lord.[7]

> "'Do not turn to mediums or spiritists; do not
> seek them out to be defiled by them. I am the Lord
> your God.'" (Lev. 19:31)

> "'As for the person who turns to mediums and
> to spiritists, to play the harlot after them, I will also

---

7. Several good resources on this topic are Merrill F. Unger, *Demons in the World Today*
(Wheaton, Ill.: Tyndale House Publishers, 1971); Elizabeth L. Hillstrom, *Testing the Spirits*
(Downers Grove, Ill.: InterVarsity Press, 1995); Clinton E. Arnold, *Powers of Darkness:
Principalities and Powers in Paul's Letters* (Downers Grove, Ill.: InterVarsity Press, 1992); and
Russ Parker, *Battling the Occult* (Downers Grove, Ill.: InterVarsity Press, 1990).

set My face against that person and will cut him off from among his people.'" (20:6)[8]

These statements come from One who knows these things better than we ever could. Occult activities carry a high price tag—and they are easy to embrace, but not so easily released.

Second: *God is dishonored by pursuits of the future apart from His Word.* When opportunities arise to peer into the future, our curiosity makes them difficult to resist. But when we look to sources like astrology and tarot cards, it is like slapping God in the face, because He asks us to trust only Him for our future.

Third: *God is delighted when we turn to His Word and trust Him only.* This may seem far less exciting than contacting the spirit world, but when you turn to the Lord, you honor His evaluation of a whole sphere of illegitimate activity. Your rejection of any occult involvement acknowledges that He knows best, and you wisely steer clear of satanic turmoil and danger.

Living Insights

Are you aware of how specific God's commands are concerning occult involvement? He told Israel before they entered the Promised Land:

> "When you enter the land which the Lord your God gives you, you shall not learn to imitate the detestable things of those nations. There shall not be found among you anyone who makes his son or his daughter pass through the fire, one who uses divination, one who practices witchcraft, or one who interprets omens, or a sorcerer, or one who casts a spell, or a medium, or a spiritist, or one who calls up the dead. For whoever does these things is detestable to the Lord; and because of these detestable things the Lord your God will drive them out before you. You shall be blameless before the Lord your God." (Deut. 18:9–13)

---

8. Other key references to the occult are Deuteronomy 18:9–13; Isaiah 47:8–15; Jeremiah 10:1–5.

The Lord's command holds true for us today.

Many people—Christians included—get involved in occult activities, thinking that they're fun and harmless things to do. But harmless and powerless they are not. To remain unaware of that truth is to leave yourself frighteningly unprotected against Satan's deadly games.

Have you allowed the occult to make even the smallest inroad into your life? Perhaps you've never sought out a medium, but do you read your horoscope—just for kicks? Do you visit the fortuneteller at the county fair? Do you bring out the Ouija board or tarot cards to spice up a party? Write down and bring into the light any areas of darkness you are playing with.

_____

_____

Has your involvement affected you or others? How?

_____

_____

_____

Do you fully realize the character of the Evil One, who is behind these activities? Read John 8:44, 1 Peter 5:8, and Revelation 12:10, 12, and write down his true nature.

_____

_____

_____

Do you really think he just wants you to have a little harmless fun? He who prowls about like a roaring lion seeking whom he may devour most certainly has more in store for you than that. So don't leave yourself open and vulnerable to this deceitful enemy. He may appear as an angel of light (2 Cor. 11:14), but in him is immeasurable darkness.

With this in mind, then, commit yourself to staying away from any involvement with the occult. Throw away your Ouija board, tarot cards, and all other paraphernalia. Stop reading your horoscope. Do whatever you have to do to close the door on this area.

And keep your children away from occultic harm too.

Out of your protective eye, your children can be innocently drawn into this realm through simple games and experimentation with their playmates. Their curious, exploring minds are wonderful gifts—but they need loving guidance to keep them out of harm's way.

If you discover that they have already experimented with the occult, stay calm and respond in a caring, balanced way. They don't need to be shamed for being curious; they need to be protected from Satan gaining a foothold in their minds.

God wants the best for us and our children—this is what's ultimately behind His "no" to the occult. Remember what He's told us:

> "'For I know the plans that I have for you,' declares
> the Lord, 'plans for welfare and not for calamity to
> give you a future and a hope.'" (Jer. 29:11)

God offers a future with hope—something Satan would never do. So don't play his games. He doesn't play by your rules.

 Questions for Group Discussion

1. Ahaziah never learned, did he? He had seen the Lord act in his parents' lives. He had watched the prophecies about his father's defeat and death come true. And he knew that two companies of soldiers he sent out were immolated at Elijah's word—yet he still sent a third! What qualities of the heart *prevent* people from seeing and learning?

2. What qualities *help* people learn from God's dealings with themselves and others?

3. Are there areas where you've been a little slow to learn? What do you think keeps the lessons from sinking in? How has God shown His patient grace in continuing to try to teach you?

4. Ahaziah deliberately sought knowledge from a supernatural power other than the Lord. Why was the Lord so offended by this?

5. Have you ever dabbled in the occult? How and why? Did you realize you were turning away from God in doing so? What was the short-term result? What has been the long-term effect?

6. Have you asked God to release you from any occult entanglements that still have you bound? Do you realize how much God loves you and wants you freed from Satan's power? Take some time to read aloud the following verses: Psalm 102:18–22; 146:7; Isaiah 61:1; Acts 26:17–18; Romans 6:22–23; Galatians 5:1; Colossians 1:13–14; Hebrews 2:14; 1 John 3:8b; 4:4.

7. What can you do to guard your children from the lure of the occult? Do you know what TV shows and movies they watch? What books they read? What kind of music they listen to? What sites on the Internet they visit? What can you tell them about Satan's intentions versus the Lord's desires for them?

Chapter 10

A NO-DEATH CONTRACT
2 Kings 2:1-14

Much had changed for Elijah since his despairing flight into the wilderness (1 Kings 19). His anxiety for God's work had turned into a more calm, patient faith that God's will would be done with or without him. He rested in the Lord's use of other spokesmen, even helping guide and teach groups of prophets at Bethel and Jericho (2 Kings 2:3, 5). And he felt confident that God's work would go on after him through his successor, Elisha.

When we enter 2 Kings 2, then, we see an Elijah who had fought the good fight, kept the faith, and was about to finish his course. He would receive God's commendation, "Well done, good and faithful servant!"—not in words but in a striking display of God's power. For Elijah didn't age gracefully and then quietly die; he stepped from earth to heaven in one miraculous, deathless stride!

Let's join Elijah one last time, following him to his appointment with eternity and watching the Lord provide for His people with Elisha.

Elijah's Final Journey

How did Elijah spend his last day on earth? By journeying with Elisha to reflect on Israel's more faithful past and to strengthen God's other prophets one more time.

Gilgal: The Place of Beginnings

> And it came about when the Lord was about to take up Elijah by a whirlwind to heaven, that Elijah went with Elisha from Gilgal. Elijah said to Elisha, "Stay here please, for the Lord has sent me as far as Bethel." But Elisha said, "As the Lord lives and as you yourself live, I will not leave you." So they went down to Bethel. (2 Kings 2:1-2)

Elijah and Elisha left from Gilgal, which was a place of historic beginnings for Israel. Here the infant nation took its first steps into the Promised Land—through the miraculously dry bed of the parted Jordan River (Josh. 4). Gilgal was their beachhead, their place of security and safety. It was also a place of remembrance. Twelve stones from the middle of the dry riverbed were made into a monument to memorialize what the Lord had done for them there. Finally, Gilgal was a place of consecration—Israel had to perform the covenant sign of circumcision before venturing further into the land (5:1–9), and then they observed their first Promised Land Passover, eating the food of Canaan rather than the wilderness manna (vv. 10–12).

Crossing the Jordan and preparing at Gilgal were Joshua's first missions after succeeding Moses. In retracing those early steps of Israel, Elijah might have had that historic succession in mind, as well as his own handing off of God's work to Elisha. Paul R. House observes that this scene at historic Gilgal emphasizes "the continuity of God's message and God's messengers in Israel's history and places Elijah on a par with Moses."[1]

Interestingly, Elijah gave Elisha the chance to stay comfortably in Gilgal instead of trekking with him to Bethel. But Elisha's steadfast refusal proved that "his commitment to Elijah and Elijah's ministry was unfailing."[2]

Bethel: The Place of Communion

When they reached Bethel, the company of prophets pulled Elisha aside and asked him,

> "Do you know that the Lord will take away your master from over you today?" And he said, "Yes, I know; be still." (v. 3)

Loyal to his master, Elisha asked the prophets not to remind him of Elijah's soon departure. Perhaps their words added to his own sorrow at losing this mentor and mighty man of God, or maybe Elisha felt it was disrespectful to speak of it in Elijah's presence. Or it might have been that Elisha didn't want to interrupt Elijah's thoughts, which may have turned back to Bethel in the times of Abraham and Jacob.

Abraham had built altars at Bethel, which in Hebrew means "house of God," when he first set out for Canaan and when he

---

1. Paul R. House, *1, 2 Kings*, The New American Commentary Series (Nashville, Tenn.: Broadman and Holman Publishers, 1995), p. 257.

2. J. Robert Vannoy, note on 2 Kings 2:2, in *The NIV Study Bible*, gen. ed. Kenneth L. Barker (Grand Rapids, Mich.: Zondervan Bible Publishers, 1985), p. 525.

returned after a sojourn in Egypt (Gen. 12:8; 13:3–4). But it was Abraham's grandson Jacob who had the most awesome experiences there. Bethel was where the Lord visited Jacob in a dream, with angels ascending and descending a ladder between earth and heaven. In that night vision, the Lord reiterated His promise to Abraham and made it personal to Jacob:

> "I am the Lord, the God of your father Abraham and the God of Isaac; the land on which you lie, I will give it to you and to your descendants. Your descendants will also be like the dust of the earth, and you will spread out to the west and to the east and to the north and to the south; and in you and in your descendants shall all the families of the earth be blessed. Behold, I am with you and will keep you wherever you go, and will bring you back to this land; for I will not leave you until I have done what I have promised you." (28:13–15)

Jacob regarded Bethel as "the gate of heaven" (v. 17), and he, too, set up an altar there (vv. 18–22). God directed him to return to Bethel years later, after He had made Jacob rich, and He reassured him that His earlier promise stood firm (35:1–15).

How Elijah must have yearned for Israel to remember and re-commit to the Lord's gracious covenants! It must have saddened him to think that his people had chosen Baal's empty words over the Lord's faithful promises, to blend in with the nations rather than bless them. But it also must have encouraged him to recall the Lord's enduring words to Jacob: "I am with you . . . I will not leave you" (28:15).

Jericho: The Place of Victory

Once more, as if testing Elisha's commitment to the Lord's call, Elijah said to him,

> "Elisha, please stay here, for the Lord has sent me to Jericho." But he said, "As the Lord lives, and as you yourself live, I will not leave you." So they came to Jericho. (2 Kings 2:4)

Elisha again refused to choose the easy way over following God's man. So he and Elijah journeyed to Jericho together, where the prophets there asked Elisha the same question that those at Bethel had: "Do you know that the Lord will take away your master from over you today?" (v. 5a). Elisha gave them the same answer: "Yes, I know; be still" (v. 5b). And as Elijah and Elisha lingered in that ancient city, perhaps their thoughts returned to a glorious time in Israel's past.

The conquest of Jericho was Israel's first victory over the Canaanites and their idolatrous religion. The Promised Land was being claimed for those who followed God's will and kept His covenant—the Lord's Law, not any false religion, was to rule this land. The battle of Jericho was a holy war, and its success depended on Israel's faithfully obeying the Lord's instructions, which they did, and the Lord toppled the city's walls (Josh. 6:1–20).

The battle of Jericho was the first of many, and more were soon to come. Elijah, too, had fired off the first volleys against Baalism, and it would take many more spiritual warriors after him to finally crumble its hold on Israel.

The leading warrior in the battle against Baal would be his successor, Elisha, whose commitment Elijah appeared to test again: "Please stay here, for the Lord has sent me to the Jordan" (2 Kings 2:6a). But again Elisha's devotion remained steadfast: "As the Lord lives, and as you yourself live, I will not leave you" (v. 6b). So Elijah and Elisha proceeded to the Jordan.

The Jordan: The Place of Transition

Fifty prophets from Jericho watched Elijah and Elisha as they stood on the banks of the Jordan, providing a witness for Elisha's succession (v. 7). And what they witnessed was incredible! Like Moses at the Red Sea,

> Elijah took his mantle and folded it together and struck the waters, and they were divided here and there, so that the two of them crossed over on dry ground. (v. 8)

Commentator Thomas Constable notes that with this reminiscent display of God's power, "Elisha was reminded that the same God with the same power [as in Moses' time] was still alive and active in Israel."[3] Significantly, it was on this side of the Jordan,

3. Thomas L. Constable, "2 Kings," in *The Bible Knowledge Commentary*, Old Testament edition, ed. John F. Walvoord and Roy B. Zuck (Colorado Springs, Colo.: Chariot Victor Publishing, 1985), p. 540.

across from Jericho, that Moses died and was buried by God (see Deut. 32:48–50; 34).[4] And like Moses, this is where the Lord would take up Elijah.

With the time drawing near, Elijah asked Elisha if there was anything he wanted from him (v. 9a). Elisha named his request: "Please, let a double portion of your spirit be upon me" (v. 9b). What exactly was Elisha asking here? Richard D. Patterson and Hermann J. Austel explain:

> The enormity of the loss of Elijah, that spirit-filled and empowered prophet, must have so gripped the humble Elisha that, claiming his position as first born, he asked for the firstborn's "double portion" [see Deut. 21:17]—that is, for especially granted spiritual power far beyond his own capabilities to meet the responsibilities of the awesome task that lay before him.[5]

This was a wise and reverent request from the man who was heir to Elijah's prophetic role. But it was beyond Elijah's power to give, so he left it in the Lord's hands:

> "You have asked a hard thing. Nevertheless, if you see me when I am taken from you, it shall be so for you; but if not, it shall not be so." (v. 10)

You can bet that Elisha didn't take his eyes off his master after that! And it's good he didn't, because suddenly, "a chariot of fire and horses of fire"—symbols of God's power—came between the two men, and "Elijah went up by a whirlwind to heaven" (v. 11). Like Enoch, Elijah didn't see death (Gen. 5:24); and like Jesus, he went to heaven with his disciple looking on (Acts 1:9).

How different Elijah's "non-death" was from Ahab's bloody end, as Paul R. House observes:

> The contrast between the deaths of Elijah and his enemies could hardly be any more stark. Elijah, the

---

4. See T. R. Hobbs, *Word Biblical Commentary: 2 Kings* (Waco, Tex.: Word Books, Publisher, 1985), vol. 13, pp. 20–21.

5. Richard D. Patterson and Hermann J. Austel, "1, 2 Kings," in *The Expositor's Bible Commentary*, gen. ed. Frank E. Gaebelein (Grand Rapids, Mich.: Zondervan Publishing House, Regency Reference Library, 1988), vol. 4, p. 176.

faithful servant of God, ascends to heaven. Ahab and Jezebel, the sworn enemies of Yahwism and the prophets, die at the hands of their foes. God's word continues unchecked, while the wicked receive the consequences of their actions. Baalism will not prevail.[6]

But was Elisha granted his request? Did he see Elijah as the Lord took him to heaven? He surely did:

> Elisha saw it and cried out, "My father, my father, the chariots of Israel and its horsemen!" And he saw Elijah no more. Then he took hold of his own clothes and tore them in two pieces. (v. 12)

Elisha saw Elijah as the nation's true strength—its chariots and horsemen—because of his unswerving commitment to bring the people back to Yahweh, the one true God. Elijah's departure was the nation's loss as well as his own, and Elisha mourned him by tearing his clothes.

But by tearing his clothes, Elisha also renounced his former life and prepared to take up the prophetic mantle:

> He also took up the mantle of Elijah that fell from him and returned and stood by the bank of the Jordan. (v. 13)

Staring at the Jordan with Elijah's mantle in his hands, Elisha might have remembered the Lord's words to Joshua before he crossed that river on dry land: "This day I will begin to exalt you in the sight of all Israel, that they may know that just as I have been with Moses, I will be with you" (Josh. 3:7). Would the same be true for him? Elisha sought God's confirmation in the sight of the fifty witnesses:

> He took the mantle of Elijah that fell from him and struck the waters and said, "Where is the Lord, the God of Elijah?" And when he also had struck the waters, they were divided here and there; and Elisha crossed over.
>
> Now when the sons of the prophets who were

---

6. House, *1, 2, Kings*, p. 210.

at Jericho opposite him saw him, they said, "The spirit of Elijah rests on Elisha." And they came to meet him and bowed themselves to the ground before him. (2 Kings 2:14–15)

Where was the God of Elijah? He was with Elisha now, and a whole new era of reaching out to the Lord's people with power and truth had begun.

Lessons from the Journey

God's care and honor of His good and faithful servant, as well as the provision of His presence for a new generation, teach us at least two lessons.

First, *when a person of God dies, nothing of God dies.* Although Elijah didn't die, he was taken off the scene. But God was still there; His plan was still moving forward. The same holds true today. All of us are part of God's plan, but we aren't the plan itself. The Lord remains committed to His people's welfare, and He will provide the leaders we need to guide us in His way.

Second, *when the work of a great person is finished, the beginning of another is started.* Elijah had been taken home, but the Lord had Elisha in the wings for a long time. Elisha's ministry would not be the same as Elijah's, but it would reflect the way God wanted to communicate His message to His people at that time. Though we grieve when an era has passed under one person's leadership, we can watch with hope and excitement to see what God will do in the next.

Living Insights

We've come a long way from Cherith, haven't we? Let's use the outline from our chapter to retrace Elijah's steps, pausing to reflect on what we've learned from his experience and our own in each place.

The Place of Beginnings

The beginning is where we put our roots down. The roots of Elijah's faith grew deep in the Lord through watching His promised drought come to pass, through relying on His provision at Cherith and Zarephath, and through praying for His miraculous revival of the widow's son. What have you learned about Elijah through these episodes? What insights have you gained about God?

_____

_____

_____

_____

_____

_____

Where did the roots of your faith grow deep in the Lord? What did He reveal about Himself to you?

_____

_____

_____

_____

_____

The Place of Communion

Elijah most certainly met with God at Cherith and Zarephath, but his experience at Mount Sinai brought him closest to God. What did Elijah's weakness teach you about faithful servants of God? Did you gain a new perspective about the Lord from this story?

_____

_____

_____

_____

_____

Do times of crisis drive you to the Lord? When Jacob fled Esau, he found encouragement in God's promises to him at Bethel. Which of the Lord's promises do you need to rest on?

_____

_____

_____

_____

_____

_____

The Place of Victory

Elijah experienced God's overwhelming victory over Baal on Mount Carmel. Yet victories don't come without battles. What was at stake on Mount Carmel? What role did prayer play in the struggle?

_____

_____

_____

_____

_____

_____

What have been some of your greatest battles in life? How have you tried to fight them? How often has prayer been part of your plan? What victories has God given you?

_____

_____

_____

_____

_____

The Place of Transition

Elijah had run his leg of the race; at the Jordan River, it was time to pass the baton to Elisha. Sometimes transitions come about because of death—when Moses died, Joshua led the people into the next era of salvation history. What do both of these stories reveal about God's care and control? How did God show how much He valued the person who served Him wholeheartedly?

Good-byes sometimes feel a little like dying, don't they? What have been some major transitions in your life? Have you had to "die" to something or someone? How has the Lord helped you reach the end, and what new beginnings has He brought you to?

Because of Elijah's commitment to the Lord and his openness to do whatever the Lord asked, he became the "chariots" and "horsemen" of Israel—the spiritual strength of his nation. The faithful prophet had more power than the king and queen, not because of any strength in himself, but because of God's power in him.

We, too, can bring spiritual strength to our nations when we commit ourselves to doing the Lord's will as revealed in His Word. May these studies from Elijah's life encourage you to follow more closely the one true God and love more dearly the people He seeks to save.

Questions for Group Discussion

1. Why do you think the author of 1 and 2 Kings wanted to highlight how much Elijah was like Moses? How is this significant? What's the importance of Elisha being likened to Joshua? What do you learn from these parallels?

2. What does Elisha's request for a "double portion" of Elijah's spirit reveal about him? For example, do you see humility? Or presumption? Or an awareness of his need as Elijah's successor? Why do you think he asked for this?

3. Are you ever afraid to ask the Lord for "big things" in your desire to serve Him? Why? What does Elisha's example teach you?

4. Why do you think the Lord took Elijah up in a whirlwind, accompanied by fiery chariots and horses? What is the Lord trying to tell us with this picture?

5. Has God ever brought someone along to pick up your work where you left off? How did you feel toward this person? Threatened? Grateful? Humbled? Did you help equip them for the job, as Elijah did with Elisha (2 Kings 2:9a)?

6. What's the most important insight you've gained from your study in Elijah's life?

BOOKS FOR
PROBING FURTHER

If you would like to explore further the world of the prophets and kings; dig deeper into the life of Elijah; see how the Lord used his successor, Elisha; and learn how God can use you in the battle against modern-day Baals, we recommend the following books.

Bimson, John J. "1 and 2 Kings," in *New Bible Commentary: 21st Century Edition*. 4th ed., rev. Gen. ed. D. A. Carson, R. T. France, J. A. Motyer, G. J. Wenham. Downers Grove, Ill.: InterVarsity Press, 1994.

Dillard, Raymond B. *Faith in the Face of Apostasy: The Gospel according to Elijah and Elisha*. The Gospel according to the Old Testament Series. Phillipsburg, N.J.: Presbyterian and Reformed Publishing, 1999.

Hobbs, T. R. *Word Biblical Commentary: 2 Kings*. Vol. 13. Waco, Tex.: Word Books, Publisher, 1985.

House, Paul R. *1, 2 Kings*. Vol. 8 of The New American Commentary Series. Nashville, Tenn.: Broadman and Holman Publishers, 1995.

Kaiser, Walter C., Jr. *Have You Seen the Power of God Lately? Lessons for Today from Elijah*. San Bernardino, Calif.: Here's Life Publishers, 1987.

Provan, Iain W. *1 and 2 Kings*. New International Biblical Commentary Series. Peabody, Mass.: Hendrickson Publishers, 1995.

Rice, Gene. *Nations under God: A Commentary on the Book of 1 Kings*. Grand Rapids, Mich.: William B. Eerdmans Publishing Co., 1990.

Robinson, J. *The First Book of Kings*. The Cambridge Bible Commentary Series. London, England: Cambridge University Press, 1972.

———. *The Second Book of Kings*. The Cambridge Bible Commentary Series. London, England: Cambridge University Press, 1976.

Roper, David. *Seeing Through: Reflecting God's Light in a Dark World*. Sisters, Ore.: Multnomah Books, 1995.

Swindoll, Charles R. *Elijah: A Man of Heroism and Humility.* Nashville, Tenn.: Word Publishing, 2000.

Wallace, Ronald S. *Readings in 1 Kings.* Grand Rapids, Mich.: William B. Eerdmans Publishing Co., 1995.

Zacharias, Ravi. *Can Man Live without God.* Dallas, Tex.: Word Publishing, 1994.

Some of these books may be out of print and available only through a library. For those currently available, please contact your local Christian bookstore. Books by Charles R. Swindoll, as well as some books by other authors, may be obtained through Insight for Living.

Insight for Living also offers Bible study guides on many books of the Bible, as well as on a variety of issues and biblical personalities. For more information, see the ordering instructions that follow and contact the office that serves you.

NOTES

NOTES

NOTES

NOTES

NOTES

ORDERING INFORMATION

ELIJAH

If you would like to order additional Bible study guides, purchase the audiocassette series that accompanies this guide, or request our product catalogs, please contact the office that serves you.

United States and International locations:

Insight for Living
Post Office Box 69000
Anaheim, CA 92817-0900

1-800-772-8888, 24 hours a day, seven days a week
(714) 575-5000, 8:00 A.M. to 4:30 P.M., Pacific time, Monday to Friday

Canada:

Insight for Living Ministries
Post Office Box 2510
Vancouver, BC, Canada V6B 3W7

1-800-663-7639, 24 hours a day, seven days a week
infocanada@insight.org

Australia:

Insight for Living, Inc.
20 Albert Street
Blackburn, VIC 3130, Australia

Toll-free 1800 772 888 or (03) 9877-4277, 8:30 A.M. to 5:00 P.M., Monday to Friday
iflaus@insight.org

World Wide Web:

www.insight.org

Study Guide Subscription Program

Bible study guide subscriptions are available. Please call or write the office nearest you to find out how you can receive our Bible study guides on a regular basis.